The Origins of Single-Session Therapy

This book explores the single-session work done by Sigmund Freud and considers the implications of this work for the current theory and practice of single-session therapy (SST).

While contemporary interest in SST can be traced to Moshe Talmon's (1990) book, its origins go back to Freud. There are three cases in the literature where Freud can be said to practise SST, and this is the first book that examines these cases in one place and without getting caught up in the intricacies of Freudian theory. Windy Dryden first explores the three cases in which Freud conducted single-session work with patients. Particular attention is paid to the third patient, Margarethe Lutz, who discussed the session in an interview. This work is important because it is the only client-based view of Freud conducting therapy that lasted a single session. The book closely examines the work of Freud in these sessions and tracks how it impacts the development of SST.

This book will be of interest to any single-session practitioners, as well as those scholars and followers of Freud.

Windy Dryden is in part-time clinical and consultative practice and is an international authority on rational emotive behaviour therapy and SST. He has worked in psychotherapy for more than 50 years and is the author and editor of over 290 books.

Routledge Focus on Mental Health

Routledge Focus on Mental Health presents short books on current topics, linking in with cutting-edge research and practice.

The Knowledge of the Psychoanalyst
Raul Moncayo

Elements of Faith: Psychoanalytic Phenomenon and Lived Experience
Brent Potter

The Power of Being a Subject: Transcending Myth and Machine
Matthew H. Bowker

Psychoanalysis and the Wisdom of Ecclesiastes: A Time to Heal
Paul Marcus

Critical Consciousness: Beyond Impasses in Environmentalism, Psychoanalysis, and Education
Joseph Scalia III and Lynne S. Scalia

The Origins of Single-Session Therapy: An Examination of Freud's Single Sessions
Windy Dryden

For more information about this series, please visit: www.routledge.com/Routledge-Focus-on-Mental-Health/book-series/RFMH

The Origins of Single-Session Therapy

An Examination of Freud's Single Sessions

Windy Dryden

Routledge
Taylor & Francis Group
LONDON AND NEW YORK

First published 2026
by Routledge
4 Park Square, Milton Park, Abingdon, Oxon OX14 4RN

and by Routledge
605 Third Avenue, New York, NY 10158

Routledge is an imprint of the Taylor & Francis Group, an informa business

For Product Safety Concerns and Information please contact our EU representative GPSR@taylorandfrancis.com. Taylor & Francis Verlag GmbH, Kaufingerstraße 24, 80331 München, Germany.

British Library Cataloguing-in-Publication Data
A catalogue record for this book is available from the British Library

ISBN: 9781041072621 (hbk)
ISBN: 9781041072669 (pbk)
ISBN: 9781003639633 (ebk)

DOI: 10.4324/9781003639633

Typeset in Times New Roman
by Newgen Publishing UK

Contents

Preface

There are three cases in the literature where Freud can be said to practice single-session therapy (SST). While contemporary interest in SST can be traced to the publication of Moshe Talmon's (1990) book, *Single-Session Therapy: Maximizing the Effect of the First (and Often Only) Therapeutic Encounter*, its origins go back to Freud. These three cases require examination, and this is the first book to do so in one place.

When I first thought of writing about Freud's SST cases, I was going to include them in a book where two famous therapy figures, one living, Irvin Yalom, and one dead, Sigmund Freud, set out to see people for a single therapeutic consultation.[1]

In beginning this project, it quickly became apparent to me that to include the single-session work of both legendary figures in one volume was unworkable for three main reasons. First, when Freud did his sessions (1893 with Aurelia Kronich,[2] 1910 with Gustav Mahler,[3] and 1936 with Margarethe Lutz[4]), there was nothing written about SST and Freud, himself, did not refer to this aspect of his work in any special way. By contrast, in 2020, Yalom had access to a burgeoning literature on SST, which he chose not to consult (Dryden, 2025a), even though he referred to his work as 'single-session consultations'. Second, in addition, Freud wrote up only one of his three single sessions (the one with Aurelia Kronich[5]). Yalom, by contrast, wrote up all the consultations in *Hour of the Heart* himself, with help from his son, Benjamin (Yalom and Yalom, 2024). Finally, I considered the book would be lopsided as I would be considering three single sessions in Freud's case and 22 in Yalom's. Consequently, I decided to write separate books on Freud's single-session work (this volume) and Yalom's single-session work (Dryden, 2025a), and Routledge kindly contracted both books.

Let me be clear about what I am *not* going to do in this book, before I discuss what I am going to do. I am not going to get caught up in psychodynamic interpretations of Freud's work with AK, GM and ML. First, this is not my area of expertise, and there are those far more knowledgeable in this area who can address this (e.g., Appignanesi and Forrester, 2005; Slavin and Rahmani, 2016; Swales, 1988). Second, this type of analysis does not necessarily shed light on what happens in a single session. From a SST perspective, there is no correct way of interpreting the material. What I will do, by contrast, is to consider Freud's work from the perspective of SST while being mindful, as I said above, that he would have had no access to such literature during the period, 1893–1936, when he conducted these sessions because none existed.

It is my hope that this book achieves two goals: first, that it demonstrates how Freud conducted SST, and second, that it places SST within a historical context.

If both Freud and Yalom were prepared to offer single-session consultations to patients,[6] I hope that this will encourage present-day therapists to do the same.[7]

Windy Dryden,
London and Eastbourne
September 2025

Notes

1 Yalom had been experiencing ongoing and ever-increasing problems with his memory. On 31 March 2020, he announced to his Facebook followers that 'I've stopped my ongoing therapy practice but am still continuing to see individuals via Zoom or Skype for one or two consultations of an hour and offer whatever I can to be helpful, including, if indicated, a suitable referral'. His book *Hour of the Heart: Connecting in the Here and Now* (Yalom and Yalom, 2024) discusses 22 of over 300 of these single-session consultations.

2 Referred to as AK in this book.

3 Referred to as GM in this book.

4 Referred to as ML in this book.

5 Named 'Katharina' by Freud in *Studies in Hysteria* (Freud and Breuer, 1895). I will follow the stance taken by Appignanesi and Forrester (2005) and refer to her by her real name, Aurelia Kronich (AK here).

6 Both Freud and Yalom referred to the people who sought help from them as patients.

7 With suitable training and supervision.

1 What Is Single-Session Therapy?

The major focus of this book is three single sessions that Sigmund Freud did with people over a 43-year period. In my view, these sessions can be seen as the origins or precursors of single-session therapy (SST), as it was later developed by Moshe Talmon, Michael Hoyt, and Robert Rosenbaum, three psychologists who worked at the Kaiser Permanente Clinic in Northern California (Talmon, 1990). In discussing these three sessions, I will do so as they relate to modern SST. However, and this is important, it is not my intention to indicate what Freud should have done in these sessions from an SST perspective. He did what he did, given the knowledge he had at the time. However, I will outline what a single-session therapist might have done if they had conducted the session.

To put what I have to say in context, it is important that I outline what SST is. In doing so, I will bear in mind that the book's focus is on Freud's work.

The Nature and Foundations of Single-Session Therapy

In this section, I will discuss the nature of SST and the ideas that it is based on. I will begin with a definition of SST.

Single-Session Therapy: A Definition

> Single-session therapy is an intentional endeavour where the therapist and client contract to collaborate to help the client achieve their desired outcome by the end of the session. This is with the full understanding that, once the client feels they have gained

DOI: 10.4324/9781003639633-1

the maximum benefit from the session – after reflecting on their learning, processing it, applying it, and observing the results – additional support is available at a later date if needed. However, single-session therapy also includes the situation where the client and therapist agree to meet once and once only.

SST: Planned or Unplanned

SST can be planned as defined above or unplanned. When SST is unplanned, the client decides to only attend for a single session when both were contracted to meet for a number of sessions. When this happens, the client may have got what they wanted from the first session and decided that they did not need any more help, as occurred in the majority of Talmon's (1990) 200 cases of unplanned SST clients whom he surveyed. However, it may also mean that the client has not benefited from the first session and decides not to attend further agreed-upon sessions based on their experience of the initial encounter.

When considering the three single sessions that Freud conducted that are described in this book, in the cases of AK (Aurelia Kronich) and GM (Gustav Mahler), the unspoken expectations of both seemed to be that they would only consult Freud once. In the case of ML (Margarethe Lutz), my reading of the situation was that Freud quickly determined that because of the demeanour of ML's father, he would probably not see her again and thus had to make an impact in that one session (see Chapter 4).

What's in a Name?

The term single-session therapy is often taken to mean a therapy that lasts for a single session, and this was the case in Freud's work with AK, GM and ML. However, as my definition provided above shows, SST does not preclude the possibility that a person may get more help later if they choose to seek it.

To reflect both possibilities, I use the term ONEplus therapy instead of SST. This term makes explicit the fact that the therapist and client will work to help the latter take away what they have come for from that session ('ONE') and that more help is available later to the client if they need it ('plus').[1]

Even a Brief Encounter Can Be Therapeutic

SST is predicated on the idea that even a brief encounter between two people can yield therapeutic benefit for one of them. This was particularly the case for ML who 75 years after seeing Freud for a single session still attested to the benefits of that session.

Therapy Takes Exactly the Length of Time Allocated to It

One of the questions I am often asked about SST when I teach on the subject is how long the session is. People who appraise SST using a conventional therapy mindset often think that the session has to be longer than the traditional 50 minutes. In my experience, the session is often less than 50 minutes. I inform my single-session clients that the session will be up to 50 minutes, which means we can end the session when the work is done, rather than when the clock dictates.

A recent development in the field concerns what has been called microtherapy or microcounselling. Here, a person is offered a very brief opportunity of around 20 minutes to speak to a counsellor on a specific issue. While people can access several of these microtherapy sessions, they often choose to utilize one. If they require additional help later, it is usually related to a separate issue. While it may seem, at first glance, that little of value can be achieved in twenty minutes, in reality, much can be done. As pointed out by Applebaum (1975), therapy takes exactly the time allocated to it.

While we do not know how long Freud's conversation was with AK, we do know that his session with ML lasted 45 minutes and his session with GM lasted about four hours.

The Modal Number of Sessions Clients Have is '1' and the Majority of People Who Attend for One Session Are Satisfied

In therapy agencies, the most frequent number of sessions clients have is '1' followed by '2', followed by '3', and so on, and the majority of people who attend for one session are satisfied with it. (Brown and Jones, 2005; Hoyt and Talmon, 2014; Young, 2018). Certainly, Freud's three patients each seemed satisfied with the single conversation that they had with Freud.

The Power of Now and This Is It

All a single-session therapist knows for certain is that they are with the client in the present moment and that this may be the only opportunity that they have to help the person. Consequently, they 'seize the moment' and get down to business straight away. Both AK and GM consulted Freud when he was on holiday, and it was unlikely that they would then become a regular patient of his. ML was brought to see Freud in his consulting room by her father, who, at the beginning of the consultation, spoke for her daughter. When Freud asked ML's father to wait in his waiting room, he complied but showed his displeasure. As already noted, in my opinion, Freud decided that it was unlikely that her father would let ML see Freud again, and consequently, he had one shot to help her.

The Power Is in the Client

In general, a single-session therapist considers that their initial role is to encourage the client to use their own power and that of their environment to help themself. Thus, they help the client to connect with their internal strengths, identify and utilize past instances when they were able to help themself with their nominated[2] and other problems and draw upon any external resources that may assist them. If these sources do not yield results, the single-session therapist will likely offer their expertise to assist the client with their nominated issue, drawing on their preferred therapeutic approaches in doing so.

Freud made little attempt to discover any of his three single-session patients' strengths, past abilities to solve emotional problems or available environmental resources. What he did do with AK and GM was utilize his own knowledge about factors that accounted for the presence of these two patients' emotional problems, helping them gain insight into these dynamics so that they could make sense of them.

With ML, I think Freud saw that he had one opportunity to become a memorable presence for her, countering the malevolent influence of her father, and he took it. As we will see, she grew up lonely and lived out a fantasy life in her bedroom. Her father used to take her to the cinema but led ML away when the scenes got a little 'racy'. ML wanted to stay and watch the film. Freud asked her to think of him in the battle between what she wanted to do – stay and watch the film and what her father wanted for her – leave the cinema. Freud was saying to her, I am the expert here, and I support you in what you want to do.

In different ways, Freud's practice in these single sessions was as an expert, giving reasons for maladaptive responses in the cases of AK and GM and giving expert guidance in the case of ML.

I believe that the source of Freud's expertise was different for each patient. For AK, it was because Freud was a doctor. In 1893, when the meeting between AK and Freud took place, Freud was not celebrated, and even if he were famous, I doubt whether AK would have known about him. For GM, on the other hand, I think the source of Freud's expertise was that he was a celebrated doctor. For ML, the source of Freud's power and resultant expertise was that he effectively stood up to her father.

In summary, Freud's practice in these three single sessions was based on the idea that the power is in the therapist rather than in the client.

More Is Less, and Less Is More

In SST, the therapist is advised to do only enough work with the client to enable them to take away something meaningful with respect to their nominated issue. Many therapists new to SST think that, as they may have only one session with the client, this means that they must give the person as much help as possible. When they do this, it has the opposite effect. The client, overwhelmed by excessive information about their problem and suggested remedies, ends up retaining very little. Thus, in SST, we say 'more is less' and 'less is more'. From the accounts of Freud's three single sessions, he ensured that he did not overload his patients. With AK and GM, he gave them enough to make sense of their problems, which seemed helpful to both. With ML, Freud gave her a discrete task to say in the cinema when her father wanted her to go and to think of him as she did so.

Sooner Is Better

In SST, we argue that the closer the help provided to a person when they seek it, the better. With AK, Freud had a helping conversation with her when she asked to speak with him. He could have declined, saying he was on holiday. He could have arranged to talk to her at a later date. He did neither of these things. He acted on the 'sooner is better' principle.

With GM, Freud offered him three sessions, which he cancelled. Freud gave him one last opportunity, which GM took. So, Freud could have helped GM more quickly, but the fact that he didn't was wholly due to GM.

With ML, it is not clear what the gap was between when she was referred to Freud and when he saw her. However, that did not seem to have much bearing on what happened in the session itself and the dramatic impact it had on ML.

Something Meaningful Can Come from the Session for the Client

Therapists who look at SST with a conventional therapy mindset are sceptical that anything meaningful can happen in a single session with a therapist. However, those of us experienced in this mode of therapy are often surprised by what clients can take away from single sessions when they report back to us that they have learned[3].

With AK, the impact of the session on her remains unknown. Appignanesi and Forreseter (2005: 107) noted that after some family fallout when AK told her mother what had happened with her father (see Chapter 2), she fell in love with Julius Ohm, a local forest manager. They married on 26 September 1895, and moved to Julius's employer's estates, 300 miles away in Hungary. Their first child was born in 1896, with five more following between 1897 and 1905. Although her marriage was happy, Aurelia felt isolated in Hungary. She returned each summer to the Ottohaus on the Rax, which her brother took over in 1903. She died suddenly there on 3 September 1929, of a heart attack likely caused by excess morphine prescribed by the local doctor for her severe pain.

With GM, his wife told us her husband impulsively decided to consult Freud because he realized he had lived the life of a neurotic and that he was concerned that his wife would rebel against the fact that he withdrew sexually from her. When they finally met, Freud and GM had a four-hour 'walk-and-talk' conversation in Leiden, Holland.

The outcome of this session, according to Kuehn (1965: 358), was that

> Freud's diagnosis and reassurance seemed to be very helpful. At least no more was heard of the manifest problem throughout the remaining eight months of Mahler's life. Indeed, the memories and letters are full of endearments, closeness and warmth in the relationship which the couple had seldom approached in the earlier

years of their marriage. But there are shadows in the background as we recall Alma's previous comment: 'I knew my life was utterly unfulfilled. I concealed all this from him ... we played out the comedy to the end.'

With ML, we have a clearer understanding of what she took away from the session with Freud, as we have her own account of the session and its aftermath. As I will discuss more fully in Chapter 4, she seemed to take away a determination to stand up to her controlling father and did so successfully. While she may have done this anyway later, as she described herself as rebellious, Freud gave her encouragement to do so at a difficult time for her.

Who Is Single-Session Therapy For?

In modern SST (see Chapter 5), proponents of this mode of therapy delivery argue that it is for anybody who wants to avail themself of it. As Bobele and Slive (2025) argue, there should be no barriers to seeking help when it comes to SST. Indeed, as the contributors to their book demonstrate, SST is best viewed as open access, allowing clients to access one hour of therapy at their convenience during the facility's operating hours. When SST is by appointment, this should take place as soon as possible after the client has chosen a convenient time.

As I say in my training workshops, SST should not be offered to clients who don't want it and should not be practised by therapists who don't want to practise it.

Indeed, Freud did not use any exclusion criteria before offering single-session help to his three patients. With AK and ML, he helped them at the first opportunity. He also did so with GM, but because the latter had made and cancelled three appointments, Freud stipulated that if GM cancelled the fourth appointment, then he, Freud, would not see him.[4]

The Importance of the Working Alliance Between Therapist and Client in Single-Session Therapy

One of the most frequently asked questions about SST concerns whether it is possible to develop a good enough relationship in a single session (Dryden, 2022). The consensus among modern-day

SST therapists is that the answer is a resounding yes, and research appears to support the importance of the therapeutic alliance in determining the outcome of a single session (e.g., Simon et al., 2012). In this section, I will consider the question of the relationship between client and therapist in SST from the perspective of working alliance theory, introduced by Ed Bordin (1979) and developed by me (Dryden, 2006, 2011). I will not refer to the working alliance between Freud and his three single-session patients in this section but will do so in the appropriate chapter when I consider the work that Freud did with each patient.

The Four Constituents of the Working Alliance

Bordin's (1979) seminal article on the working alliance proposed three constituents of the alliance: the bonds between therapist and client, the goals of therapy, and the tasks each person undertakes in the service of helping the client achieve their goals. Since first being introduced to this concept in 1978, it has been one of the most important ideas that has informed my work as a therapist, particularly latterly as a single-session therapist (Dryden 2025b). However, from the outset, I considered that it was lacking in one crucial respect. It neglected the understandings that have to be made between the client and the therapist concerning therapy. So, I proposed a fourth constituent of the working alliance that I called 'views' (see Dryden, 2006, 2011).

I will discuss each constituent separately presently in the chapter. Bringing them together, I would say:

> A good working alliance occurs when the therapist and client have a good enough collaborative bond, share views on matters related to the client's problems and their remediation, agree on the goals of therapy, and agree on the tasks needed to help the client achieve their goals. Such agreements can be either explicit or implicit.

Bonds

'Bonds' refer to the interpersonal connectedness between the therapist and the client.

There are three different dimensions to this connection. The first is attributed to the work of Carl Rogers (1957) and concerns the extent to which the client experiences the therapist as empathic, respectful and genuine in their encounter. These are known as 'core conditions'. The second concerns the extent to which the therapist and client are collaborating on the tasks of therapy, rather than one person doing the work and the other not. The third concerns the therapist's influence base. Does the client listen to and is influenced by the therapist because of the latter's likeability or their expertise?

Views

As mentioned earlier, views refer to the understandings between therapist and client concerning matters therapeutic. With respect to SST, these involve the following agreements i) that the person will meet the therapist for a single session and work to take away from the session what they have come for knowing that they can have more help if they request it; ii) the nature of the client's problem and iii) what will best help the client deal with their problem.

Goals

As Mahrer (1967) pointed out many years ago, the goal of therapy is twofold: to alleviate suffering and promote development. Single-session therapy usually has the first objective, while single-session coaching usually has the second (Dryden, 2020). In this book, we are concerned with the former, as this was the nature of Fried's work with AK, GM and ML. When thinking of goals in SST, it is vital to consider what is realistic and what is unrealistic. It is usually unrealistic to expect that we can solve a client's problem in its entirety in a single session, but it is realistic to help them find a solution which they can implement later.

Tasks

Tasks are activities that the therapist and client carry out in the session and, in the client's case, after the session, to help the client achieve their therapeutic goal. It is important that the client and therapist agree to carry out their respective tasks and that the client understands the purpose of the therapist's tasks. Such an agreement and understanding are usually implicit, and problems in this constituent part of the working alliance tend to appear when a client indicates that they don't understand what the therapist is doing and don't understand what they are supposed to do in therapy.

Notes

1 I will use the term 'single-session therapy' in this book for two reasons. First, it is the most commonly used term in this therapeutic space, and second, each of Freud's clients only saw him once.
2 In this book, I refer to the problem the client wants to discuss as the 'nominated' problem.
3 In SST, we often do not know what the client has taken away from the session because they do not come back to see us. When Talmon (1990) contacted 200 of his clients who attended one session with him, despite the agreement that therapy would last longer, he found that 78 per cent of this group were satisfied with the help they received.
4 When SST is offered in an open-access, enter-now service, there are no cancellations since no appointments are made.

2 Freud and Aurelia Kronich

The Session

While holidaying in the Rax mountains[1] in August 1893, Freud was approached by the 18-year-old, rather sullen-looking daughter of an innkeeper where he was staying. Her name was Aurelia Kronich (AK here).

AK began by asking Freud if he was a doctor and noted that she knew this because he had written it in the visitor's book. She asked whether he could spare some time to talk to her, as her nerves were quite bad. She mentioned that she had previously consulted a doctor who prescribed something for her nerves, but it did not help.

So, we know that AK had sought help before. In SST, we would ask about this so that we could encourage the client to utilize anything helpful from such help and discourage them from using anything that was not helpful. Freud shows no interest in AK's previous experience of seeking help. She also indicates a strength in being able to ask a stranger to help her when he was on vacation, which she must have known about. In SST, we would acknowledge this as a strength and, at some point, see if AK could use this to help herself.

Freud concluded that AK's problem was neurotic and acted accordingly. He first asked AK what she was suffering from, and she replied breathlessness, which could become so severe that she thought she was suffocating. Freud then invited AK to sit down and concentrated on her breathlessness. When Freud focused on the symptom that AK chose to highlight, he was adopting a patient-centred focus that is typical in SST.

AK then described to Freud her symptoms, including pressure on her eyes, a heavy head, a dreadful buzzing, giddiness, a crushing

DOI: 10.4324/9781003639633-2

sensation on her chest, a tight feeling in her throat and a pounding in her head. In response to Freud's question about whether she felt frightened during these episodes, AK stated that at those moments she believed she was going to die and dared not go anywhere, contrasting this with her usual bravery. She also thought at the time that someone was standing behind her, about to grab her. AK's bravery is another of her strengths, which SST therapists would make use of later. Freud did not do this.

Freud had heard enough to diagnose AK's problem as a hysterical attack characterized by anxiety. He then asked her if she had any thoughts or images at that moment. She replied that she always saw a terrible face that looked at her in a frightening way, which made her afraid. At this point, Freud believed he was getting to the core of the issue, but AK then said she did not recognize the face and did not know where the attacks originated from, although she mentioned that she first experienced them two years ago. Freud concluded that, since he was unable to carry out an analysis, a simple conversation might still prove effective.

Freud then decided to draw on his observations that anxiety in young girls was often experienced by them when their pure minds were first confronted with the world of sexuality.

Freud began by asking AK for her views concerning where her anxiety came from, and when he drew a blank, he offered AK his view. Freud did so as an expert, which I think impressed his young patient. His intervention was theory-driven.

Freud told AK, 'If you don't know what it is, then I'll tell you where I think your attacks come from. Once during that time two years ago, you saw or heard something that embarrassed you very much, that you would rather not have seen' (Freud and Breuer, 2004: 130). AK replied, 'Heavens, yes. I caught my father[2] with the girl, Barbara[3], my cousin' (Freud and Breuer, 2004: 130).

In response to Freud's enquiry concerning how AK knew about her father's affair with Barbara, AK told Freud that one day, while she was searching for Barbara, she saw her father lying on top of Barbara. AK immediately turned away from the scene, felt breathless, kept her eyes tightly closed, and experienced pounding in her head. She said she did not know what frightened her.

Freud then said to AK that if she could remember what was going on inside her when she had her first attack, and what she was thinking when it happened, that would be the end of her troubles. Here again, Freud used his expertise this time with suggestion.

Freud then asked AK about the head she saw whenever she was breathless, but she said it was not Barbara's or her father's, and as this line of enquiry led nowhere, Freud asked AK what happened then. She said that she was ill for a few days, got sick a few times, and couldn't stop thinking about what she saw. Freud interpreted her illness as disgust, which she felt when she looked into the room. AK agreed that she must have felt disgusted (is she being compliant here?), but does not know why.

Freud encouraged AK to continue speaking freely about whatever came to mind, and she recalled telling her mother about what she had seen after her mother confronted her about keeping something hidden. Later, following some tough moments, her mother left her father and took the family to run a local inn, leaving her father with Barbara, who was now expecting a baby.

Then, AK told Freud two sets of older stories, which he said astonished him. The first set happened when she was 14, and her father twice tried to seduce her when he was drunk. She fended him off, saying it wasn't nice, and it disturbed her sleep. AK said that she did not realize at the time what her father wanted but did so only much later. On the first of these two occasions, AK said that she felt her father's body, by which I presume she meant his erect penis.

When asked by Freud if she had experienced the breathlessness she had previously, AK. replied that she felt a sensation of pressure on her eyes and chest, although not as intensely as when she had found her father with Barbara.

The second set of stories concerned AK becoming aware that there was something between her father and Barbara. She claimed that while she may have been frightened, she did not make anything of these occasions.

After sharing these two stories with Freud, AK appeared relieved, even exalted, and Freud gained clarity about what had transpired. Having seen through the window her father and Barbara engaging in intercourse, AK immediately connected this to her belief that her father wanted to have sex with her, which she rejected. What followed was what Freud called a period of incubation or 'working-out', where vomiting serves as a substitute for disgust. She was not repulsed by witnessing her father with Barbara, but by the memory of what Freud termed the nocturnal assault, when she felt his erect penis (referred to by Freud as 'the body of her father', or 'uncle' in the text). Subsequently, during the session, AK indicated – though did not explicitly state – that Freud was correct; however, the unspoken agreement between them was that Freud's interpretation was accurate.

Later in the conversation, AK said that the head in her hallucination was her father's, but not from that time. It stemmed from her father's rage against her since he blamed her for the divorce and angrily pursued her whenever he saw her afterwards. The face was her father's, twisted with rage.

Freud ended the case by saying, 'I hope that talking things through with me in some way benefited this girl whose sexual sensibility had been wounded at such a young age; I did not see her again' (Freud and Breuer, 2004: 136).

In his analysis of the case, Freud made the following two points:

1. The case was solved more by guesswork than by analysis.
2. The patient acknowledged everything that Freud interpolated into her report as likely to be true. Still, she was not in a position to recognize it as something that she had experienced.

The Outcome of the Session

It is sometimes not possible to know what the outcome of a single session has been for the client. However, whenever possible, attempts should be made to discover such an outcome. This was what Talmon (1990) did when he contacted 200 of his unplanned single-session cases. In Freud's day, single-session conversations were rare and thus, follow-ups were not done. This was so in the case of two of Freud's three single-session 'patients' whom he saw while he was on holiday (AK and GM). In the case of ML, we are fortunate to have her account of the session and its aftermath.

In the case of AK, we know that in 1895, two years after her encounter with Freud, she fell in love with and married a man with whom she had six children and a relatively happy and untroubled life in the Hungarian countryside. However, as she often experienced loneliness, she would return each summer to the Ottohaus on the Rax, which her brother had taken over in 1903. AK died there, suddenly, on 3 September 1929, of a heart attack, aged 54.

On reflecting on the outcome of the session for AK, Sabbiadini (1992: 168) said,

> Did Freud 'cure' Katharina? He never alleged that he did. In fact, no psychoanalyst would believe that a single 'therapeutic consultation', such as that offered impromptu to Katharina by Freud, could

permanently resolve a patient's problems. Psychoanalysis, by its nature, involves detailed exploration, interpretation and working-through of the analysand's material and, more specifically, of transference and countertransference phenomena as they progressively emerge in the course of the therapeutic process, within a carefully structured setting. This process is more likely to require years of intense daily sessions on the couch in the analyst's consulting room than a one-off conversation on a mountaintop. We cannot altogether dismiss, however, the possibility that the meeting with Dr Freud had a powerful and long-term effect on Katharina. What we know about Aurelia Kronich's mental health is that, although she occasionally went through periods of loneliness and sadness and of common unhappiness, she never again required professional help for her psychological difficulties. Perhaps her nerves, after all, were not too bad.

Reflections on Freud's Single Session with AK: Therapeutic Factors

Freud had a single-session conversation with AK in 1893, three years before he formally developed psychoanalysis. His work with AK stands in sharp contrast with the lengthy treatment associated with this form of treatment. In this section, I will offer my reflections on the discussion that Freud had with AK.

In my book on Irvin Yalom's single-session conversations (Yalom and Yalom, 2024), I noted that he argued that the main therapeutic factor that accounted for the gains that his patients made was due to the here-and-now connection that he formed with them during their single sessions (Dryden, 2025a). As Yalom often said in that book and more generally of his work, 'It's the relationship that heals.' However, I noted the presence of other therapeutic factors at play that may have been important in determining what his patients derived from speaking with him. I have done the same for this book. What follows, then, are my views on the therapeutic factors that could have been at play in leading to the benefits derived by AK from discussing her issue with Freud.

Help at the Point of Need

As mentioned in Chapter 1, people often remark when having had a planned single session with a therapist that they appreciated being seen quickly. This is particularly the case when the person enters an open-access service which offers help in that visit. What happened with AK is that, having ascertained that Freud was a doctor from the visitor's book at the hotel where he was staying and where she lived, she followed him on one of his walks, asked for help and got it immediately. As I mentioned earlier in this book, Freud could have flatly refused her request for help, saying that he was on vacation, or he could have agreed to talk with her, but at a later time and date at his convenience. He did neither. He offered to help AK at *her* convenience. I think that getting help from a doctor at the point of her need was a therapeutic factor for AK.

The Working Alliance Between Freud and AK

Writing from a psychoanalytic perspective, Sabbiadini (1992: 164) said the following about the relationship between Freud and AK:

> I imagine that in their conversation Katharina already unconsciously experienced Freud as a transferential object, as the 'good' doctor/father/husband who could help her grow into a healthy, non-neurotic, sexually mature young woman, while her 'bad' father had been responsible for her somatic symptoms, for her psychological difficulties, for her 'unhappy look', and for her cousin Barbara's[4] illicit relationship and out-of-wedlock pregnancy.

Looking at the case from a working alliance perspective, I note the following.

The Bond Between Freud and AK

It seems to me that AK drew great comfort from being able to tell Freud what her problem was, from the fact that he took her seriously and gave her his undivided attention. As it unfolded, their relationship seemed to be based on AK's respect for Freud as a doctor. She looked up to him as a result. There is no indication that AK sought out Freud because he had a special interest in hysteria, so in this case, Freud was, for her, a very fortunate choice of doctor.

Freud capitalized on AK's trust in him and adopted the role of an expert, confident in the correctness of his pronouncements. Here are three examples of Freus's expertise in action:

- 'I'll tell you where I think your attacks come from. Once during that time two years ago, you saw or heard something that embarrassed you very much, that you would rather not have seen', to which AK is seemingly very impressed: 'Heavens, yes', she replied (Freud and Breuer, 2004: 130).
- 'Fraulein ... If you could remember now what was going on inside you when you had your first attack and what you were thinking when it happened, it would be the end of your troubles', to which AK responds: 'Yes, if I only I could ...' (Freud and Breuer, 2004: 131).
- 'I know now what you were thinking to yourself when you looked into the room. You were thinking: now he's doing with her what he wanted to do with me on that night and on the other occasions. That's why you were disgusted, because you remembered the sensation when you woke up in the night and felt his body', to which AK responds: 'That may well be, that that was what I was disgusted by and that that was what I thought' (Freud and Breuer, 2004: 131).

Social psychologists (e.g. Strong and Claiborn, 1982) argue that therapists can have influential power over their clients because of their likability (i.e., 'I will listen to you and trust you because I like you') or because of their expertise (i.e., 'I will listen to you and trust you because you are an expert'). Clearly, Freud influenced AK because she saw him as an expert, a role he capitalized on. In influencing her, Freud helped her to understand her previously unexplained symptoms, and this understanding did seem to have a substantial impact on her.

Views

When AK decided to seek help from Freud, it is difficult to know what was in her mind. However, I guess that she probably did not expect to see Freud again after their conversation. There is evidence, however, that Freud saw this as a single session and did not expect to see AK again either. Indeed, Freud says at the end of his account of their session, 'I hope that talking things through with me in some way benefited this girl whose sexual sensibility had been wounded at such an early age. I did not see her again' (Freud and Breuer, 2004: 136).

It seems to me that the entire session that Freud had with AK was predicated on the notion that as she had little or no conscious understanding of why she experienced her symptoms, Freud offered her such a view. He told her that the reason she was disturbed by the sight of her cousin having intercourse with her father was the realization that this is what he wanted to do with her in the episodes that she recounted to Freud. She accepted Freud's view. She also came to understand that the face she dreaded seeing was her father's face, contorted with rage, whenever he saw her afterwards, because he blamed her for the breakup of his marriage.

Goals

There was no discussion between Freud and AK concerning her goals for seeking him out that day. Traditionally, one visited a doctor because one had unexplained symptoms, hoping that the symptoms would cease, if not at the end of the consultation, then later. In physical medicine, this would usually be achieved by the patient being given some medicine to take or undergoing a medical treatment. In AK's case, her 'medicine' was the relationship she had with Freud and the understanding she was offered that explained her symptoms. We do not know if the cessation of her symptoms was achieved. All we know is that she lived a relatively happy life and that she did not seek further therapeutic help.

Tasks

In situations like this, the primary task for the patient is to inform the therapist about their symptoms, answer the therapist's questions and engage in the ensuing conversation. AK did all these things openly, which indicated the trust that she placed in Freud. As Sabbiadini (1992) noted, Freud's tasks in the session included listening attentively to AK, asking her questions to clarify her symptoms and to test his theory about what happened to her, linking her symptoms to past traumata and translating her somatic symptoms into their symbolic emotional equivalents (e.g. 'being sick means disgust'). How important the content of Freud's interpretations were in helping AK is not known. All we know is that they seemed to make sense to her from Freud's account (Freud and Breuer, 1895, 2004). It could be that she would have accepted alternative interpretations from Freud as long as they made sense to her.

One thing worth noting is that after telling Freud about her experiences with her father and her father's sexual experiences with her cousin, AK's reaction was thus: 'She is as if transformed: the sullen, suffering face has come to life, her eyes are bright, she is relieved, exalted' (Freud and Breuer, 2004: 134). This response came *before* Freud's interpretation linking these two stories, suggesting that therapeutic benefit came more from AK's tasks (in this case, disclosure and getting things off her chest) than from Freud's tasks (making interpretations, etc.).

Conclusion

From my perspective, AK benefited from her conversation with Freud, as it occurred in a 'help at the point of need' context. She was able to openly discuss her symptoms and later her experiences with her father, including his sexual encounters with her cousin. She was able to do this because she trusted and respected Freud. AK accepted Freud's assessment of her problem, partly because it helped her understand her symptoms, which had previously been unexplained, and partly because she trusted Freud's expertise and accuracy and because he took her seriously and listened attentively to her.

Notes

1 Rax is one of the most famous mountains in the Northern Limestone Alps, located near Vienna.
2 'Uncle' in the original.
3 Barbara was the real name of AK's cousin. Freud changed this to Franziska.
4 See note 3.

3 Freud and Gustav Mahler

Unlike the session with AK, where Freud gives us a clear sense of what happened during their meeting, there is little available detail of what happened in the single session that Freud had with GM on 26 August 1910 in the Dutch spa town of Leiden. What we do know about this meeting comes from i) an article by Kuehn (1965), ii) Alma Mahler's (1946) biography of her husband, Gustav, iii) a diary entry by Marie Bonaparte reporting on what she was told by Freud in 1925 about the meeting, iv) a letter that Freud wrote to Theodor Reik in 1934, v) a few pages in Ernest Jones' (1955) biography of Freud and vi) the Wikipedia entry on Mahler.[1]

Given that GM was a famous orchestra conductor and music composer, much more is known about him than about either AK or ML. As such, some context is in order before I consider the session itself.

Gustav Mahler and Alma Mahler

John Kuehn (1965), the author of a key article on the encounter between Freud and GM, as he calls it, says that in general, 'Mahler's childhood was painful, anxiety-provoking and mournful in the clinical sense. Yet in a crucial way, there were more significant assets in the parent-child relations than are readily identifiable. Above all, there was consistent concern manifested by both parents for their prodigious son' (Kuehn, 1965: 349).

GM was 41 when he met Alma Schindler, 22, and they married just weeks later. Unlike his authoritarian approach at work, GM's home life was characterized by a deep need for reassurance, a childlike dependence and a desire for excessive attention from his wife. He was

DOI: 10.4324/9781003639633-3

only truly at ease with his two daughters (Kuehn, 1965: 351). GM's relationship with his wife was quite complex. When they married, GM demanded that his wife give up her own ambitions as a composer and devote herself to him, becoming a housewife and later a mother. This effectively meant she had to give up her social life, which she loved so much.

However, although she loved GM, his self-preoccupation and withdrawal from her sexually had its toll. In 1910, while at a spa resort with her second daughter, Alma met a young German architect, Walter Gropius, who fell in love with her. After eight years of marriage with GM characterized by privation, restraint and austerity, Alma responded to the young man's attention, who allowed her to be the passionate woman that she was and that she had lost touch with. They begin a brief, torrid affair.

After Alma returned from her trip, Gropius wrote her a love letter, but seemingly in error, addressed it to GM. When he discovered her affair, GM confronted her, and she told him that she wouldn't leave him but that she was desperately unhappy.

Thijs de Wolf[2] writes about GM and Alma's relationship thus:

> Mahler could not be without his Alma, and she couldn't live without him, but when their intimacy grew, their fear grew, too, and then both would literally or figuratively take a step back. If then the distance grew too big, and separation would threaten, on that side, the fear would grow again. It seems as if it had to be all or nothing, of life or death, of merging and disappearing inside the other or losing each other. One could almost say that the only more or less satisfying, fruitful and living relationship Mahler could have was the one with his music. He was able to surrender to this, to his music.

This was the context surrounding GM's decision to seek out Freud.

The Making and Cancelling of Three Appointments

GM contacted Freud when the latter was on holiday with his family near the spa town of Leiden. Freud was irritated because, by that time, he did not want to see patients during his vacation. However, because of GM's fame, he agreed to see the composer. However, during a short period, GM made and cancelled three appointments to see Freud. Ernest Jones (1955) attributed this to GM's '*folie de doute*' of his obsessional neurosis. GM's wife said it was because he was ill and preoccupied with his work on his tenth symphony (Mahler, 1946). However, other reports (e.g., Kuehn, 1965) have claimed that GM was ambivalent about seeing Freud. Part of him wanted to because his wife was dissatisfied and complained about the withdrawal of his libido, while the other part of him feared that seeing Freud would have a negative impact on his musical creativity. Whatever the reason, it was only when Freud told GM that he was leaving the area soon and would not be able to see him that GM made a fourth appointment, which he kept.

The Session

The meeting point was at In den Vergulden Turk, an apartment building in Leiden. However, according to Ernest Jones (1955), Freud's biographer, the two men decided to 'walk and talk' and they spent four hours discussing GM's issues in the streets and parks of Leiden during which, according to Jones, 'a kind of psycho-analysis' took place.

So, what do we know about what happened in the session and what may have been helpful?

Kuehn's (1965) Article and Jones's (1955) Account

In 1965, Kuehn published an article entitled 'Encounter at Leyden: Gustav Mahler consults Sigmund Freud', and much of what we know about the sessions comes from this source and from Ernest Jones's (1955) brief account of the meeting.

Kuehn (1965) notes that the two men discussed extensively the richness of GM's experience. During this conversation, a remark by Freud greatly influenced GM: 'I take it your mother was called Marie. I should surmise it from various hints in your conversation. How comes it that you married someone with another name, Alma, since your mother evidently played a dominating part in your life?' With surprise, Mahler told him that his wife's full name was 'Alma Marie', but he called her 'Marie' (Jones, 1955: 89).

Kuehn (1965: 357) states that after all this was brought to GM's awareness, he was then able to go ahead and

> abreact his fears about his marriage, his excessive suspiciousness, his inability to gratify his wife, and his unreasonable demands

> and annoying mood swings, which recently had made him even more difficult to live with. Freud confronted the composer with his attitudes and behaviour with considerable vehemence: 'How dared a man in your state ask a young woman to be tied to him? I know your wife. She loved her father, and she could only choose and love a man of his sort. Your age, of which you are so much afraid, is exactly what attracts her?' Following then in the therapeutic sequence 'to understand', 'to confront', 'to clarify' came the therapeutic insight coupled with reassurance: 'You need not be anxious. You loved your mother, and you look for her in every woman. She was careworn and ailing, and unconsciously, you wish your wife to be the same.'

In the course of the same talk, Jones (1955: 89) states:

> Mahler suddenly said that now he understood why his music had always been prevented from achieving the highest rank through the noblest passages, being spoilt by the intrusion of some commonplace melody. His father, apparently a brutal person, treated his wife very badly, and when Mahler was a young boy there was a specially painful scene between them. It became unbearable to the boy, who rushed away from the house. At that moment, however, a hurdy-gurdy in the street was grinding out the popular Viennese air 'Ach, du lieber Augustin.' In Mahler's opinion, the conjunction of high tragedy and light amusement was from then on inextricably fixed in his mind, and the one mood inevitably brought the other with it.

Freud's Letter to Theodor Reik

Unlike the session with AK, which he published as a full case study in *Studien Über Hysterie* (Freud and Breuer, 1895), Freud wrote very little about his session with GM. However, he did write a letter about the session briefly in response to a query from Theodor Reik, who asked Freud about his meeting with GM. In that letter, Freud said the following:

> I analysed Mahler for an afternoon in the year 1912 (or 1913)[3] in Leyden. If I may believe reports, I achieved much with him at that time. This visit appeared necessary to him because his wife

> at the time rebelled against the fact that he withdrew his libido from her. In highly interesting expeditions through his life history, we discovered his personal conditions for love, especially his Holy Mary complex (mother fixation). I had plenty of opportunity to admire the capability for psychological understanding of this man of genius. No light fell at the time on the symptomatic facade of his obsessional neurosis. It was as if you would dig a single shaft through a mysterious building. (Kuehn, 1965: 355)

Wikipedia

According to the entry on Mahler in Wikipedia, Mahler appeared to gain some comfort from his meeting with Freud. The entry states:

> One of Freud's observations was that much damage had been done by Mahler's insisting that Alma give up her composing. Mahler accepted this and started to positively encourage her to write music, even editing, orchestrating and promoting some of her works. Alma agreed to remain with Mahler, although the relationship with Gropius continued surreptitiously.

The Outcome of the Session

Freud's diagnosis and reassurance appeared to be very effective. According to Freud himself and to Kuehn (1965), no further mention was made of the manifest problem throughout the remaining eight months of GM's life. Indeed, the memories and letters shared between GM and his wife were filled with endearments, closeness and warmth in the relationship, which the couple had rarely explored in their earlier years of marriage. There is also some indication that GM decided, after speaking with Freud, to encourage his wife to resume her own musical interests, having put an end to them once they had married. However, there were what Kuehn calls dark shadows. The following statement from Alma demonstrates this: 'I knew my life was utterly unfulfilled. I hid all this from him … we played out the comedy to the end' (Kuehn, 1965: 358). This shows that what might be regarded as a good outcome by the patient and the patient's therapist may not be regarded as such by the patient's wife.[4]

It is not clear what the impact was of GM's insight in linking the noble with the commonplace in his music on his subsequent work since, as we have seen, he died eight months after consulting Freud.

Reflections on Freud's Single Session with GM: Therapeutic Factors

When AK consulted Freud in 1893, we have Freud's case-study account of this meeting, and thus, it is possible to infer the presence of therapeutic factors at play in that consultation (see Chapter 2). As we shall see when I discuss Freud's session with ML, which took place in 1936, we are privileged to have the patient's account of this meeting 70 years after it took place (see Chapter 4). However, with GM, while we have quite a lot of detail of GM's relationship with his wife and the events that led to the consultation, we have little detail about what happened in the consultation itself, other than what I have already discussed.

Given that there is little published about the long consultation between Freud and GM, and that they were both celebrated in their own field, there have been two major attempts to fictionalize what may have occurred between the two of them. Thus, we have a 2010 German film directed by Felix and Percy Adlon called *Mahler auf der Couch*[5] which came out a century after the actual consultation, and we have a novella *Mahler's Mater Dolorosa*, in which the author, Martin van Amerongen (1992), tries to reconstruct Freud and Mahler's walk. As both are works of fiction, I decided not to consult them, as they are not reliable guides as to what transpired on that walk, however entertaining they may be.

Nevertheless, it is possible to speculate about the potential therapeutic factors at play during the consultation.

The Working Alliance Between Freud and AK

The Bond Between Freud and GM

In 1925, Freud told his pupil Marie Bonaparte (1882–1962) about the meeting with Gustav Mahler. Her diary makes it obvious that GM and Freud immediately understood each other. GM was 50 years old and Freud was 54. There were similarities in the men's lives. Both spoke German (with regional colouring), and had the same social, historical and cultural background from Vienna; both had an international reputation, had been in America, studied Philosophy, were fascinated by Dostoyevsky, and had a morbid fear of death.

If Freud and GM formed a strong bond during their walk, this similarity would have been the breeding ground for its development. We also know that Freud was impressed with how quickly GM appeared to understand psychoanalysis, having had no previous contact with it. This may have warmed Freud to GM.

We are given no reason why their session lasted for four hours. My hunch is that it had something to do with the bond the two of them had formed and how impressed Freud was with GM's understanding of his ideas. Also, the work that Freud did with GM was wide-ranging, with GM telling Freud his life story despite having a narrower focus concerning his purpose in consulting Freud (i.e., his lack of potency with his wife). While GM may have been ambivalent about seeking help, once he became comfortable with Freud, he seemed quite willing to share his life with Freud, and this took time.

It seems to me that a very important therapeutic factor here lies in the fact that GM had Freud's undivided attention for four hours and could talk about anything important to him.

Not that Freud was laissez-faire during their walk. Kuehn (1965) notes the vehemence with which Feud confronts GM, telling him, at one point, how dare he ask a young woman to tie himself with someone in his state. In this context, Kuehn (1965: 357) notes: 'the tremendous authority with which Freud made an interpretation or gave reassurance while at the same time displaying his intuitive sense of "rightness" of how far and how deep one need to go in a given clinical situation'. We have seen with AK, Freud adopting the role of expert, albeit in a far less vehement manner, and we shall see it again in Freud's session with ML. Being the expert is therefore a dominant theme in how Freud saw his therapeutic role, at least in his single sessions. Mahler takes Freud's vehement confrontation because, in my view, he accepts Freud as an authoritative expert.

Views

Freud was at the end of his vacation when he agreed to offer GM one last chance to see him, and GM was preoccupied with writing his tenth symphony, so there seemed an implicit agreement that they would only meet once.

GM did not seem to have ideas that explained the existence of his loss of libido for his wife, but resonated with the view put forward by Freud that his potency was affected by seeing his wife as if she were his ailing mother.

Goals

Freud did not ask GM what his goals were in coming to see him. Indeed, he did not do this with any of his three patients. Freud operated on the mindset that the patient had a problem, sought help for it, and the assumption was that their goal was to bring an end to the problem. Taking this line, GM was seeking to resolve his potency issue with his wife. To what extent was Freud successful in helping GM to achieve this? As Freud tells Reik in his 1934 letter to him: 'If I may believe reports,[6] I achieved much with him at that time', and Kuehn (1965: 358) says: 'At least no more was heard of the manifest problem throughout the remaining eight months of Mahler's life.' As I mentioned earlier, from the perspective of the presenting problem, the outcome appears positive.

Tasks

As Freud noted, GM seemed to understand psychoanalysis very quickly and appeared to resonate with the interpretations that Freud offered him concerning his mother fixation and the impact that this had on his potency. Additionally, he seemed to come to his own conclusions concerning the impact that the early experience with the hurdy-gurdy and the association in his mind between high tragedy and light amusement had, which explained why his compositions failed, in his view, to reach the highest rank. GM clearly was a good psychoanalytic patient.

In addition to offering GM interpretations linking his potency with his mother fixation, Freud used confrontation and reassurance when, on the one hand, he almost rebuked GM for asking his wife to tie herself to him when he was in such a state, while reassuring him that the reason he did so was that he looked for his mother in his wife. As I have said before, when discussing Freud's use of his authority as an expert, GM accepts and can utilize Freud's therapeutic tasks of interpretation, confrontation, and reassurance.

Conclusion

Of Freud's three single sessions, we know least about his long consultation with GM. However, piecing together the snippets that are available to us, it is possible to conclude the following. Initially, GM was ambivalent about seeing Freud, but when they did meet, they quickly 'hit it off', in large part because they had many things in common. GM quickly 'got the hang' of the ideas and method of psychoanalysis and left the session with some key insights concerning his relationship with his wife and his music. Concerning the former, GM seemed to have resolved the issue of his lack of potency through their discussions. The effectiveness of this single session, if indeed it was effective, can be attributed, in large part, to the good working alliance that Freud and GM quickly formed and developed during their long walk in the parks and streets of Leiden.

Notes

1 https://en.wikipedia.org/wiki/Gustav_Mahler.
2 https://mahlerfoundation.org/mahler/locations/netherlands/leiden/meeting-with-freud/.
3 Freud was in error about this. The session took place on 26 August 1910.
4 It may be of interest to note that after Mahler's death on 18 May 1911, in 1915, Alma married Walter Gropius with whom she had an affair that prompted GM to consult Freud. While Gropius was away on military duty, Alma met and began an affair with Prague-born poet and writer Franz Werfel in the autumn of 1917. She divorced Gropius in 1920 and married Werfel in 1929, and they remained married until Werfel died in 1945.
5 Translated as *Mahler on the Couch.*
6 It is not known to which reports Freud was referring.

4 Freud and Margarethe Lutz

The last of Freud's single sessions that I will discuss in this book concerns Margarethe Lutz, who was taken to see Freud in the spring of 1936 and was interviewed about their meeting 70 years later by Peter Roos, the interview appearing in the German weekly newspaper *Die Zeit* on 27 April 2006 with the title 'Der große Zuhörer'.

Background

In the spring of 1936, Margarethe Lutz[1] (ML), an 18-year-old young woman, was taken to see Freud by her father, who received the referral from the family doctor. ML had no idea why she was seeing Freud and was expecting to see a medical doctor because she had been suffering from bronchitis. In reality, the referral was for 'mental suffering'.

Her father sought the referral because a local coal dealer had described her as 'nuts' after seeing her, from his perspective, acting strangely in the window of the family home. In reality, what ML was doing was playing a make-believe Isolde, awaiting her Tristran. She did this because, as she said, 'I was the loneliest girl in Vienna' (Roos, 2016: 295). Her mother died in childbirth; her father remarried, but her stepmother was cold and greedy; her grandmother was very old, and her father was controlling and unapproachable.

ML was raised by her grandmother. As she told Dohler (2009):

> She still wore skirts from the 1880s, and her parenting methods were also from that time. I wasn't allowed to visit or receive anyone. I lived in isolation and was always accompanied by someone to the opera, the Burgtheater, and the dentist. My family was terribly

DOI: 10.4324/9781003639633-4

> afraid that I would be seduced. I didn't know how to seduce or be seduced. No one cared what I wanted. Sometimes I got up in the middle of the night and slept in the anteroom with my dog because he provided warmth and listened. I was terribly in need of love.

ML had no friends and was not allowed to visit anywhere without her father's permission. 'Everything that happened to me was decided behind my back and without my consent' (Roos, 2016: 295).

The Session

When they arrived to see Freud, they were taken into his consultation room, but had to wait ten minutes while Freud read the referral letter in a different room. ML's father, unaccustomed to being kept waiting, was annoyed. Cohen (2016) wondered if ML derived some spiteful pleasure from Freud putting her father in his place. Freud seemed to be saying here, 'I will do things in my way, at my place. I am in charge.' When Freud did enter the consultation room, he sat between father and daughter. Slavin (2016) argues that by doing so, Freud was communicating that they are both persons of equal value. ML remembered exactly the seating arrangements 70 years later. We can argue, therefore, that it had an impact on her. It was probably the first time anybody saw her as having equal worth to her father.

In a *Daily Telegraph* article published on 6 May 2006, ML described Freud as very frail-looking, but full of power. She said: 'It was an aged man who looked into my eyes so intently. He really took me into his gaze' (Roos, 2016: 295). He asked ML some basic questions: What was her name? Her father answered. What was her school? Her father answered. What did she do in her free time? Her father answered. What was her career ambition? Once again, her father answered. It was just like it was at ML's home. ML did not have a voice. As she said, 'I sat there silent like an object that had been brought along.'

Then, Freud matter-of-factly said to ML's father, 'Please go into the next room, I wish to speak to your daughter alone.' To ML's amazement, her father complied, but with a look of indignation on his face. As Roos notes (2016: 297): 'One simply doesn't dismiss such a father from the room, Never!' Indeed, it was the first time that ML had seen her father follow an order rather than give orders to others.

When her father had gone, Freud said to ML, '"Now it is just us together"[2] suggesting that Freud is emphasizing something that is unifying, something of oneness, of a bond between them – and something that Margarethe has never experienced before' (Cohen, 2016: 328). With those words, ML experienced a sudden lifting of pressure. Roos (2016: 296) quotes from his interview with ML:

> Her initial reticence simply vanished. And she talked and talked, and 'her constant desire to disclose myself to another person was marvellously fulfilled: Sigmund Freud was the first person in my life who really showed empathy for me who wanted to find out about me, the only one who really listened!' Unfiltered she poured out her 'hatred for her stepmother, for the school, for the Sunday walks'; that she was forbidden to have friends, could not go to the school of her choice, was not permitted to wear clothing that she liked. And then she told him that she was so imaginably lonely that all that was left for her is to act in a theater of her own fabrication, or to dress her father's chest figures in crepe paper and fantasize about the Middle Ages. 'Not once did he avert his gaze from me, and the totality of his empathy enfolded me'. (Roos, 2016: 296)

ML then went on to tell Freud that she found a key to her father's bookcase and discovered some 'spicy books' which she read avidly. Freud was interested in anything ML had to tell him, including her wish to see a love scene in its entirety when her father took her to the cinema. Roos (2016: 296) notes the following explanation was given to a baffled Freud: 'Whenever the plot veered toward intimacy between a man and a woman, her father ruled that "such things are not for you" and stood up abruptly. She was forced to leave the theater with him. Protest? Unthinkable!'

How did Freud respond? Roos (2016: 296–7) states:

> Again, 'with unbelievable attentiveness', Freud turned his benevolent eyes toward the young woman. 'His whole person was interested in me, and he thus opened something within me but no one else wanted to have opened.' Seventy years after the fact she feels the pulsing fascination and the bliss of a confidence shared. 'Suddenly I felt very contented', a feeling previously unknown to her. She was filled with a 'sense of comfort', as if she 'had just eaten an especially good meal, and then on top of it, someone had opened a window and told me, "Don't look at the floor all the time! Look out into the world! Everything is possible!"'

Before inviting ML's father back into the room, Freud looked at her deeply one last time.

> He told her that she was now 18 years old and thus an adult. And furthermore – this was less a prescription than an appeal – 'Being an adult means overcoming complaints and asserting what it means to be a person. Having desires. Contemplating dissent. Asking why things are as they are and not simply accepting everything in silence. Asserting with determination, firmness, and calm what one considers truly important'. And he prescribed in no uncertain terms, 'the next time there's a kissing scene in a movie, you stay seated!' I am telling you, 'You stay seated!' Pause. Deep Eyes. Finally, 'Have me in mind!' (Roos, 2016: 297)

In his letter to the referrer, Freud recommended activities for ML that her father could not participate in activities such as skiing and dancing, thus furthering ML's process of individuation.

The Outcome of the Session

I will now discuss the short-term and longer-term effects of the session on ML

Shortly after the session, ML went to the cinema again to watch a film where the leading male character was about to kiss the exposed shoulder of the female lead. ML's father loudly exclaimed that such things were not to be viewed by his daughter. ML did not move. Her father once again told her to come with him. ML dug all ten fingers into the armrest and pressed her bottom into the seat. 'No!', she answered, 'I'm staying put!' and she remained seated (Roos, 2016: 298). Her father went to the lobby, waited for her to come out at the end of the film and never mentioned the incident again. However, ML did not see the kiss. She had put so much into her act of defiance that she could not see the screen.

In the long term, ML followed her dream. She applied to and was accepted by the Vienna Art Academy, where she became a sculptor. Ironically, during her training, she came across the bust of Sigmund Freud that one of her teachers was working on and immediately realized who had 'saved her life', as she put it. She married in part to escape the restrictive environment in which she was living and brought up two children, during which time her art took a back seat. However, in her late eighties, she was still active as an artist, and by the time her interview with Peter Roos was published, she had recently completed a memorial plaque commissioned by the Austrian Peace Movement.

ML has consistently said that the 45 minutes she had with Freud changed her life. While this might be hyperbole, clearly it was a turning point for her. As Slavin and Rahmani (2016: 339) note:

> [ML] told Christine Dohler (2009) that her nature was such that she probably would have rebelled anyway against the authority of her family situation. But she consistently ascribed to the meeting with Freud the freedom to have her own mind throughout the challenges she confronted in the rest of her life. As she told Dohler, 'Thanks to my meeting with Freud, I led a self-determined life.'

ML realized that even without Freud's help, she would have eventually rebelled against her familial restriction and found her own way, but that Freud hastened this process. What emerged in her later interview with Dohler (2009) that did not appear in her interview with Roos (2006) was that she had a successful earlier experience of rebellion, this time against her grandmother, who was her main caregiver as mentioned above. As ML told Dohler:

> The other girls at school wore short dresses, while I wore a long skirt, revealing a hand-knitted, red petticoat. The other children teased me about it. So, I took off my petticoat and hung it on the toilet door at school. My grandmother got it from the headmaster. After that, she never forced it on me again. That was a tremendous revolution for me, but only against my grandmother, not against my father.

In modern SST as we shall see in the next chapter, we routinely ask our clients if they have had previous successful experiences of solving the very problem for which they have sought help. It is clear that Freud did not do this.

Reflections on Freud's Single Session with ML: Therapeutic Factors

In 2016, Jonathan Slavin and Miki Rahmani co-edited a special issue of the journal *Psychoanalytic Perspectives* on the single session that

ML had with Freud. Each contributor brought a distinct psychoanalytic perspective to the case and hypothesized why it had such a profound impact on ML.[3] However, we are fortunate enough to have a first-person account of the single session, and I prefer to be guided by that person in considering what was therapeutic about the session.

The Working Alliance Between Freud and ML

The Bond Between Freud and ML

In her interview with Dohler (2009), ML described Freud as 'fatherly, friendly, understanding. A friend. We constantly looked into each other's eyes, and he smiled a lot. I just talked away' (Roos, 2006: 296). ML thought that she was being taken to see a medical doctor, but adjusted quite quickly to the fact that Freud was a different kind of doctor. Freud established himself in the eyes of MK as someone strong enough to deal with her father when he answered questions directed towards her: 'Please go into the next room, I wish to speak to your daughter alone.' Then, when they were alone, Freud said to her, 'Now it is just us together'. As Cohen remarked, this was an invitation to regard their bond as a unifying one, and it has already been noted that the pressure ML experienced before her father left the room was promptly lifted.

Initially, ML was positively affected by Freud's gaze, which never lifted from her own eyes. Remember that she was a young woman whom nobody had shown an interest in, concerning what she wanted from life, either in particular or in general. ML took the opportunity afforded to her by Freud to talk, and talk she did, about a wide range of topics, including her father, her stepmother, her grandmother and her school. Freud listened intently to her with great empathy and interest, and the fact that he allowed her to express herself and her feelings about the above issues fulfilled a constant desire that she had to disclose herself to another person. 'Not once did her avert his gaze from me, and the totality of his empathy enfolded me', she told Roos (2016: 296).

Because Freud was such a good listener and genuinely interested in ML's experience, she was able to share with him her wish to see a love scene all the way to the end when her father took her to the cinema. This is when he encouraged her to refuse to obey her father the next time he decreed that they leave when a love scene came on the screen.

She was able to do this because of Freud's strong encouragement to do so and his suggestion that she keep him in mind as she did so.

In summary, my view concerning their bond, ML experienced Freud as strong enough to deal with her father, which showed ML that it was possible to assert herself with him. Freud was attentive, empathic and genuinely interested in ML. Perhaps most of all, Freud held her in his gaze as he gave her an extended opportunity to disclose herself and encouraged her to be an adult who could determine her own life, even if this meant that she had to bear discomfort as she did so.

As with his sessions with AK and GM, Freud adopted an authoritative, expert stance as he almost ordered ML to defy her father and prescribed dancing and skiing, activities that she could do on her own. These behaviours and activities were to help ML become her own person.

Views

When ML was taken to see Freud, she had no idea what kind of doctor he was. Indeed, she was surprised to find that there were not the usual trappings of a medical doctor on display. As far as I could tell, Freud did not explain to ML what he did and what kind of help he was offering. From a contemporary perspective, we would say that ML had not given her informed consent[4] to proceed with 'treatment' as she was unaware of what to expect from seeing Freud.

Freud spent the first ten minutes reading the referral letter in another room, and we have no idea of its contents. However, as soon as ML's father began to answer for her, it must have become clear to Freud that one of ML's issues was that she was not allowed a voice. Once her father left the room, ML took the opportunity to get things off her chest and tell Freud everything that she had bottled up for years. After she had done so, she mentioned that she wanted to see a love scene all the way through at the cinema. I think ML and Freud had a shared implicit view that one of her issues revolved around her lack of self-determination. Freud's later interventions reflected this shared view.

Goals

As is typical of Freud's single sessions, he did not ask what ML wanted to achieve from their conversation, but as the session progressed, her goal for self-determination emerged and as mentioned above, Freud came up with a number of ways that she could achieve this.

Tasks

As ML said in her various interviews on her session with Freud, she just talked and talked once her father had left the room (Roos, 2006; Dohler, 2009). Freud's tasks varied over the session. There seemed to be three phases to the session and Freud's tasks were different in each phase.

In the first phase of the session, Freud began by establishing his credibility with ML by asking her father to wait in another room after he answered the questions directed at ML rather than allowing ML to answer for herself.

After her father left the room, in the second phase of the session, Freud created a space where ML could feel comfortable talking to him. His attention to what she disclosed to him, characterized by an unwavering gaze, was experienced by ML as being unfolded with empathy. Freud communicated to ML during this phase that he was keenly interested in her and that her development as a person mattered to him.

In the final part of the session, Freud used a specific task to help 'kick-start' the change process for ML outside of the session. As we have seen, Freud exhorted ML to achieve her goal of seeing a love scene through to the end while at the cinema with her father by refusing to leave when he ordered her to do so. In addition, Freud suggested that he engage in activities where her father couldn't accompany her, such as skiing and dancing.

In my view, ML resonated with each of Freud's therapeutic tasks, and after the session, she implemented all three client tasks that he had suggested for her.

Conclusion

ML was interviewed by Peter Roos (2006, 2016), 70 years after she had her single session with Freud in the spring of 1936. In that interview, ML said variously that 'Those 45 minutes changed my life' (Slavin and Rahmani, 2016: 291) and 'He saved my life' (Roos, 2016: 294). During her interview with Roos (2006, 2016) and with Dohler (2009), it is clear this session has had a positive, lifelong impact on her.

We know about Freud's session with AK from Freud himself in his write-up of the case in *Studien Über Hysterie* (Freud and Breuer, 1895; 2004). We are aware of Freud's session with GM from snippets. Snippets from Freud's letter to Theodor Reik, snippets from conversations Freud had with Marie Bonaparte and snippets from Ernest Jones' (1955) biography of Freud. However, we know about Freud's session with MK from the person herself. Who else is better suited to tell us about the session and its impact? Learning from the client is highly consistent with the philosophy that underpins modern SST (see Chapter 5). Let me say unequivocally that this session is the most vivid example of the power of single-session therapy in the entire literature of SST!

Notes

1 When she went to see Freud, Margarethe's maiden name was Walter. However, she is better known by Lutz, and that is why I refer to her here as ML.

2 'Now it is just us together' is Cohen's (2016) translation of the German, 'Jetzt sind wir unterluns'. The original translation by Kenneth Kronenberg is 'Now it's just the two of us'.

3 For readers interested in psychoanalytic explanations of clinical matters, I recommend the papers in this special issue.

4 'The term "informed consent" was coined in the 1957 case of Salgo v. Leland Stanford Junior University Board of Trustees, formalizing the legal requirement to provide patients with information about risks and benefits of a procedure. However, the underlying concept of patient autonomy and the need for consent before medical intervention has roots in earlier rulings, such as the 1914 case of Schloendorff v. Society of New York Hospital, and the concept was further emphasized by international documents like the Nuremberg Code (1947) which established voluntary consent as essential for human research.' Taken from: https://www.google.com/search?q=In+which+year+did+informed+consent+start&oq=In+which+year+did+informed+consent+start&gs_lcrp=EgZjaHJvbWUyBggAEEUYOTIICAEQABgWGB4yDQgCEAAYhgMYgAQYigUyDQgDEAAYhgMYgAQYigUyDQgEEAAYhgMYgAQYigUyDQgFEAAYhgMYgAQYigUyCggGEAAYogQYiQUyCggHEAAYgAQYogQyBwgIEAAY7wUyBwgJEAAY7wXSAQoyOTY0N2owajE1qAIIsAIB8QXmZoKO4tE3tfEF5maCjuLRN7U&sourceid=chrome&ie=UTF-8.

5 The Importance of Mindset in Modern Single-Session Therapy

How Did Freud Fare?

In this chapter, I will discuss what is known as the SST mindset (or single-session thinking) that underpins the practice of what I am calling here modern SST. By this, I mean the practice of this mode of therapy delivery circa 2025 to distinguish it from the single sessions that Freud carried out between 1893 and 1936.[1]

However, when a mindset element can be found in Freud's single sessions, I will make this clear.

While I will present 47 mindset elements that together comprise the SST mindset, I do not mean to imply that a single-session therapist should keep all these elements in mind during a single session. Even if it were possible to do this, which I doubt, it would be highly disruptive of the session, given that the therapist will be thinking about mindsets rather than concentrating on the client. However, over time, with practice and supervision, these mindset elements can be internalized and will guide a therapist's behaviour in the session without the therapist having to give too much conscious thought to what they are doing.

In this chapter, thus, I will encourage therapists to *keep in mind* the mindset element I am discussing. The format I will use means that each element will begin 'Keep in mind that …'.

Keep in Mind That a Client May or May Not Know What SST Is

In modern SST practice, it is vital that the client knows what service they are getting so that they can give their informed consent[2] to proceed. If they don't know or are mistaken, then the therapist needs to

DOI: 10.4324/9781003639633-5

explain what SST is. As the principle of patient autonomy did not emerge until 1914, Freud can be excused for not seeking informed consent from AK (seen in 1893) and GM (seen in 1910). However, he did have the opportunity to explain to ML the likely nature of their session, particularly as she thought she was going to see a medical doctor.

Keep in Mind That a Client May Be Seen for One or More Sessions. Be Open to Both Possibilities

As I explained in Chapter 1, the client in modern SST is not restricted to one session, unless that is all they want. Rather, the therapist and client will work together to help the client achieve what they have come for and decide if they want more help after they have had the chance to reflect on what they have learned, digest this learning, apply it and see what happens. It is unclear from Freud's sessions with AK, GM and ML whether they could have had further sessions, but it appears from the available accounts that none of them felt the need to consult Freud again or any other practitioner, to the best of my knowledge.

The fact that Freud agreed to see AK and GM while on holiday suggests that, in his mind, these were single, 'one-off' sessions. ML was seen in Freud's consulting room, as part of his regular practice, so theoretically, he could have offered her further sessions. However, my sense is that given that he alienated ML's father by asking him to wait in the next room while he spoke to ML alone and the fact that the father was paying Freud's bill, Freud probably concluded that he would not see ML again and therefore treated the single session as a 'one-off' session.

Keep in Mind That One Session May Be Sufficient for the Client

In modern SST, the therapist thinks that the session they are having with the client may be enough for the client, given the latter's reason for seeking help. To that end, the therapist works to help the client achieve their goal, knowing that if the client needs further assistance later, it will be available to them.

Of course, we don't know what was in Freud's mind when he was endeavouring to help AK, GM and ML. We do know, however, that Freud said at the end of his write-up of his work with AK, 'I hope that talking through things with me in some way benefited this girl, whose sexual sensibility had been wounded at such a young age. I did not see her again' (Freud and Breuer, 2004: 136). This implies that he hopes their conversation was sufficient for her and that the fact that he hadn't seen her since was suggestive of this. However, it is unclear how AK would have contacted Freud if she had wanted further help.

One can argue that one of the reasons Freud saw GM for a four-hour single session was that he hoped this would be sufficient. It turned out that it was, and Mahler's libido issue with his wife seemed to be resolved.

One can also argue that at the end of his meeting with ML, Freud's exhortation to her to keep him in mind while she disobeyed her father by staying put in the cinema when a love scene came on screen was both because he thought that he would not see ML again (because her father would not sanction it) and because he did not need to see her again.

Keep in Mind That Time Needs to Be Used Wisely in SST

In modern-day SST, sessions typically last up to 50 minutes, although some therapists prefer to hold longer sessions. Regardless of the length of a single session, the therapist needs to use time wisely; otherwise, the client may not achieve what they have come for.

While we don't know how long Freud's session was with AK, his account indicates that he got down to business straight away and was able to keep the focus on his patient. It certainly seems that Freud used the time with AK wisely.

We know that Freud conducted a four-hour 'walk and talk' session with GM, but we don't know if Freud used his time wisely in this instance. Freud's letter to Reik about his session with GM tells us that Freud made 'highly interesting expeditions through his life history' (Kuehn, 1965: 355) and Kuehn (1965: 356) tells us: 'The two men ranged widely over the richness of Mahler's experience.' Jones (1955) said that Freud conducted a 'sort of psychoanalysis'. This suggests that Freud adopted a wide lens in his session with GM. However, we also know that Freud discussed specific issues such as his loss of libido with his wife, the restrictions he placed on his wife's musical interest and why he introduced commonplace tunes into his original compositions. Thus, he also adopted a narrow lens during the session. Freud's meeting with GM is not representative of modern SST, where the usual practice is to focus on a particular concern that the client wants help with. Nevertheless, Freud does seem to have achieved a great deal with GM, and even though it was a four-hour session, it is possible to argue that Freud used time wisely with his patient.

As I have pointed out, Freud's session with ML had three phases. In the first phase, Freud created a space where he and MK could have a conversation. He did this by asking ML's father to wait in an adjoining room while he and ML spoke. In the second phase, ML poured her heart out to Freud and spoke about several issues, including her dislike for school, her father and grandmother, who imposed restrictions on her, and her wish to see a love scene through to the end at the cinema. In the final phase of the session, Freud focused on this last point and exhorted MK to stand her ground when her father ordered her to leave the cinema when a love scene came on to the screen. We know that ML regarded the time she spent with Freud – 45 minutes as quoted in Roos (2006, 2016) and an hour as quoted in Dohler (2009) – as life-changing. Given the well-structured nature of the session and its exceptionally good outcome, it is possible to say, without contradiction, that Freud spent his time with ML very wisely.

Keep in Mind That It Is Useful for the Client to Be Invited to Prepare for the Session

In modern SST, the therapist invites the client to prepare for the session so that they can maximize its benefits. There is no indication in what we know about Freud's three sessions that he asked his patients to prepare for their session with him. He would not have had the time to do this in the cases of AK and ML. He would have had the time to invite GM to prepare for his session with Freud, particularly as GM had cancelled three appointments before the one that took place, but did not do so. Freud can be excused for this omission, as asking patients to prepare for their session was not standard therapeutic practice between 1893 and 1936.

Keep in Mind the Importance of Focusing on Now and That Change Is Possible Now

In modern SST, the therapist is acutely aware that they may only have one opportunity to help someone, so they need to focus on what the client wants now. They also believe that change can occur at any time, and thus, it can happen now, during the session they are currently having with their client. This mindset enables the therapist to work with the client on what they want to address now. This is the case even if the therapist thinks that the person has other, perhaps more serious issues.

From the accounts of Freud's three sessions that we have, I would say that in each case, Freud realized that he only had one chance with his patient, and therefore, he got down to work immediately and focused on their issues. The only difference here is that the modern SST therapist would have adopted a goal focus rather than a problem focus, as Freud did.

Whether Freud believed that change is possible now, there were signs that each of the patients showed signs in their respective session that a shift had occurred.

Thus, after telling Freud two sets of earlier stories concerning the abuse that she (AK) suffered from her father: 'She is as if transformed: the sullen, suffering face has come to life, her eyes are bright, she is relieved, exalted' (Freud and Breuer, 2004: 134).

In the case of GM, Kuehn (1965) tells us that he was greatly impressed with Freud's remark linking his wife with his mother. We also know that GM had the important insight into what prevented him from becoming a composer of the highest rank.

Finally, ML's account of her session with Freud shows several instances of change occurring. First, she realizes that defying her father is possible, having seen Freud request him to wait in an adjoining room. Second, she experienced a lifting of pressure when alone with Freud and gained much from being able to release her pent-up feelings while telling Freud about the restrictive nature of her life. Freud held her in his gaze throughout, and she experienced being engulfed by his empathy. Third, she agreed to assert herself when her father wanted her to leave the cinema to avoid seeing a love scene, while keeping Freud in mind. Here, she saw that change was possible and committed herself to it.

Keep in Mind That Both Therapist and Client Should Be Active in the Session and Collaborate with One Another

Much is made in the modern SST literature about the therapist and client collaborating, working together and co-creating solutions to the client's problems (for example, Dryden, 2024). The client is treated by the therapist as an equal, both actively contributing to the achievement of the client's session goal.

In his three single sessions, Freud saw himself as an expert whose job was to encourage each patient to talk to provide sufficient data for him to provide change-oriented interpretations in the cases of AK and GM and specific guidance in the case of ML. In this respect, each patient was an active contributor to the session. None of them had difficulty engaging with their task of disclosure and exploration.

There was little evidence of collaboration – as we currently conceive of the term in therapy – in Freud's sessions. The equality between the patient and therapist was perhaps most evident in Freud's lengthy walking session with GM. GM was impressed with some of Freud's insights, and Freud was impressed with GM's quick grasp and use of psychoanalysis. They shared a very similar background, and both were impressed with each other's achievements in their respective fields of work.

Keep in Mind That It Is Possible to Conduct a Session without Prior Knowledge of the Person

In conventional therapy, the therapist often receives a written referral to see a client, or if they don't, they like to take a case history to learn about the person before beginning the process of helping them. In modern SST, the therapist may not know anything about the individual beforehand unless the client has prepared for the session and shared their preparations in writing with the therapist in advance. This lack of information does not deter the modern SST therapist, as they believe it is not necessary to help someone.

In Freud's three sessions, he was faced with a different scenario in each case when it came to what he knew about the person before seeing them. He knew nothing about AK before he set about the task of helping her. He would have known who GM was by reputation, but not what problems he wanted to discuss with Freud. We know that Freud received a referral letter about ML because he spent ten minutes reading it before coming into the room where ML and her father were waiting to see him. However, we do not know the contents of the letter. Some modern SST therapists indeed prefer *not* to have any information about a client before seeing them and would not read any referral letter before the session.

Keep in Mind That the Client May Feel That They Cannot Be Helped without Certain Information Being Known about Them

Some clients come to SST wanting help quickly but don't think that they will get that help unless the therapist knows some key information about them. Consequently, in modern SST it is useful to as a client a question such as, 'Is there anything I need to know about you that if I didn't know, in your view, I would not be able to help you?'

As we have seen, Freud's practice in his single sessions was to take charge of the process and ask his clients questions that he thought were important. In his session with AK, he decided very early on that her problem was a hysterical response to having her innocent mind injured by exposure to sexual assault. His questions to her were based on this 'guess' as he called it.

With both GM and ML, there was a period when they spoke about their lives and histories in an open-ended way, and arising from this, Freud took a more specific line, leading to an interpretation concerning GM's lack of potency with his wife and guidance, and a specific task to aid ML's autonomy as an emerging adult.

Keep in Mind That Not Knowing Is a Key Part of SST

One of the struggles that a therapist new to SST faces in their practice is that there is often much they may want to know about the client that they do not know, and they do not have the time to find out. Some therapists want to find out about elements of their clients' past, while others want to know what other problems clients have so that they can help them with their most important problem. Most therapists want to know whether the session has been helpful to their clients. In the first two cases, therapists do need to focus on what their clients want from the session and this often means leaving unknown what they would like to know. In the third case, it is good practice to follow up with clients to discover the outcome of the session if they don't seek further help; however, clients often do not respond to follow-up enquiries. In all cases, tolerating uncertainty is a key therapist attribute.

As I noted above, because he took charge of each of the single sessions discussed in this book, Freud probably asked his patients anything that he felt it was important for him to know. Concerning the outcome of each session, we know the following:

1. At the end of his chapter on his session with AK, Freud remarks: 'I hope that talking through things with me in some way benefited this girl, whose sexual sensibility had been wounded at such a young age. I did not see her again' (Freud and Breuer, 2004: 136).
2. In a letter to Theodor Reik, Freud said: 'I analysed Mahler for an afternoon in the year 1912 (or 1913)[3] in Leyden. If I may believe reports, I achieved much with him at that time' (Kuehn, 1965: 355). We do not know whether Freud solicited such reports or was informed of them.
3. Finally, we do not know if Freud knew anything about the outcome of his session with ML. What does seem to be the case is that Freud seemed comfortable (in my view) about not knowing the outcome of his work, and this would have helped him become a good modern SST therapist.

Keep in Mind That Therapy Should Begin from the First Moment, if Possible

In modern SST, there is no time for therapy to be preceded by the therapist carrying out a case history, an assessment of the client or a comprehensive case formulation. Rather, the therapist begins therapy once the client has given informed consent to proceed.

How did Freud begin his session with his three single session patients? Once Freud had ascertained how AK knew he was a doctor he began therapy straight away by asking: 'What are you suffering from then?' We don't know how Freud began his session with GM, but we do know that Freud spent the first ten minutes of the session with ML (accompanied by her father) in another room reading the referral letter, which presumably the father brought with him. This may or may not be construed as Freud beginning therapy from moment one. When he did come into the room to begin the session, Dohler (2009) asked ML what questions Freud put to her. She replied:

> 'What do you do when you get home from school?' My father said, 'Nothing. She's at home and has to study.' Freud said to me, 'Are you going to a dance school?' My father said, 'That's absolutely out of the question. She's supposed to be doing her Matura exams.' Freud got fed up and said to my father, 'Please go into the next room. I want to be alone with the patient.'

When her father left the room, at that point, therapy with ML could get underway.

In conclusion, we can say that therapy began immediately with AK and immediately when Freud was finally able to see ML on her own. In the latter case, an alternative argument could be made that therapy was delayed by Freud reading the referral letter and allowing ML's father to be in the room with them at the outset. As mentioned above, we have no information about the beginning of the session with GM.

Keep in Mind That the Session Is Complete in Itself. It Is Not Necessarily the Prelude to Anything

Conventional therapists tend to view the first session as a prelude to later sessions and conduct the session accordingly. In modern SST, the therapist regards the session as complete in itself and may or may not be the prelude for further sessions. Given the possibility that the therapist may not see the client again, they tend to conduct the session accordingly.

Freud's session with AK was akin to what happens in an open-access, enter now service. The person needs help and enters a service where they can have a therapy session during that visit. After a short wait, they see a therapist who they hope can help them with the issue they are struggling with. AK followed Freud one day when he was on holiday in the Rax mountains and, having established that he was a doctor, sought help from him, which he provided on the spot. Reading Freud's account of the session, there is no indication that either Freud or AK planned to meet again. Their session can be said to have been complete in itself.

Freud's session with GM was by appointment, which eventually took place after GM made and cancelled three previous appointments. It also took place while Freud was on holiday and Freud effectively gave GM one last chance to see him before he left the area. As we know, the session lasted for four hours and was a very early example of 'walk & talk' therapy. Once again, there is no indication from what we know about the session that either Freud or GM planned to meet again. Again, the session was complete in itself.

Finally, Freud's session with ML took place in his practice towards the end of his career. I think that Freud quickly ascertained that ML's father probably would not bring his daughter back for further sessions even if they were needed, so he probably decided that he had one opportunity to help ML. As we know from her perspective, he succeeded spectacularly in this regard. Once again, the session was complete in itself.

Keep in Mind That Potentially Anyone Can Be Helped in a Single Session. But Also Keep in Mind That This Does Not Mean That Everybody Will Be Helped

In modern SST, no attempt is made to determine if a client is suitable for this mode of therapy delivery. The only criterion for proceeding with the session is that the client understands what SST is and gives their informed consent to proceed. The assumption is made that anyone can potentially be helped in a single session, but not everyone will be.

In his three single sessions, Freud did not attempt to assess the person's suitability for the work. From the outset, he got to work on helping them and hoped that what he did would be beneficial to them. As we have seen, all three patients derived some benefit from their meetings with Freud.

Keep in Mind That the Client in Front of You Is a Unique Person, and Not Representative of a Disorder

When I give training workshops on modern SST, I am often asked if this mode of therapy delivery is suitable for 'x' disorder. My response is: 'What is the person's name and what do they want from SST?' My response is to signify that in SST, the therapist views the person in front of them as a unique individual and not as representative of any disorder.

Straight from the first, Freud categorized AK as suffering from neurosis. Having ascertained that Freud was a doctor, AK said, 'I thought to myself, perhaps the doctor would have a little bit of time now – my nerves are bad, you see, and I've already been once to a doctor in L-- who did give me something, but I haven't got better' (Freud and Breuer, 2004: 128). Freud's thoughts were as follows: 'And so I was back with the neuroses again, for nothing else was likely to be the matter with this big, strong girl with her sorrowful look. I found it interesting that neuroses should flourish so well at a height of over 2000 metres, and so I questioned her further' (Freud and Breuer, 2004: 128).

While Freud did not categorize GM and encouraged him to tell his life history, which indicates that Freud responded to him as a unique person, it was Freud's work with ML which best illustrated Freud's person-centred rather than disorder-centred approach to a patient. We know this from her account of the session She said things like, 'Sigmund Freud was the first person in my life who really showed empathy for me, who wanted to find out about me, the only one who really listened!'; 'Not once did he avert his gaze from me, and the totality of his empathy enfolded me'; 'His whole person was interested in me, and he thus opened something within me that no one else wanted to have opened' (Roos, 2016: 296). It is quite clear that ML felt heard and seen by Freud, which contributed to her viewing the session as a life-changing event.

Keep in Mind That the Client–Therapist Relationship Can Be Established Rapidly

Another question that I am frequently asked in my training workshops is: 'Can a good enough therapeutic relationship be developed in SST?' (see Dryden, 2022). My answer is a resounding yes. Freud's work with all three patients showed how this was the case.

We see this especially in his work with ML, who, during a 45-minute meeting, felt seen and heard by Freud.

We also see it in his work with AK. Freud adopted an expert role with her, and she invested in the relationship because she was looking for an explanation for her troublesome symptoms.

Finally, Freud's work with GM revealed the same. Freud again took on the expert role, which helped GM understand his impotence with his wife. However, there are signs that Freud and GM are on an equal footing. Both men not only shared a similar background but also respected each other. Freud admired GM's standing in his profession and was particularly struck by how quickly GM understood psychoanalytic principles. Conversely, GM appreciated Freud's esteemed reputation and the precision of some of his interpretations.

While Freud adopted the role of expert with each of his patients, he also responded to them in different ways, showing that it is possible to develop a unique therapeutic relationship in a short period of time.

Keep in Mind That It Is Critical That You Are Transparent with Your Client

Transparency in modern SST primarily means that the therapist is clear about what SST is and what it is not, what they can do within the context and what they can't, especially within the context of the client's goals.

I don't think that there are any instances of Freud being transparent in the ways outlined above. This would have been particularly helpful to ML, who thought that she was coming to a medical doctor and was given no explanation by Freud concerning his way of working with psychotherapy patients. Also, given the fact that Freud did not specifically enquire about any of his patients' session goals, he had no reason to be explicit about what he could do with them and what he could not do.

Keep in Mind That the Client Is the Expert in Their Own Life. Thus, Single-Session Therapy Should Be Client-Led

In modern SST, the therapist's expertise primarily lies in helping the client determine what is best for them during the session. It is deemed vital that the client be encouraged to take the lead in the session concerning what they want to discuss and what they want to take away from the session. This is because they are the best person to determine what is right for them. They are the expert in their own life.

While Freud clearly adopted the role of expert with his three single-session patients, he did not view his patients as experts in their own lives and took the lead in all three encounters.

Keep in Mind That People Are Constantly Changing

Porter and colleagues (2024: 12). state that in Modern SST, 'individuals are seen as dynamic beings, constantly transforming, whether internally or due to external influences'.

Therefore, SST therapists often heed Talmon's (1990) guidance to 'Expect change. It's already well underway.' A tension exists between the therapist's mindset ('Change is occurring') and the client's perception ('I am stuck. There is no change'). A vital implication for practice is to encourage the client to move from viewing themself as stuck to recognizing that change is achievable.

I think that Freud did bring a 'change is possible' mindset to his three single sessions and worked hard with his patients to effect change. As mentioned several times in this book, Freud was successful to a greater or lesser extent in facilitating such change, which in ML's case was considerable.

Keep in Mind That the Client Decides How Much Therapy They Want

In modern SST, the client is seen as the decision-maker regarding the amount of help they want, and if they do want more help, they decide when to seek it. Because it is vital for the client to get as much as possible from their first (and perhaps only) session of SST, another appointment is only offered to the client once they have reflected on what they learned from the session, digested this learning, implemented it and then decided if they need more help (Dryden, 2024).

My sense is that Freud did not think that it was likely that he would see any of his three single-session cases again. Indeed, this issue was not discussed in the reports that we have available on these sessions.

Keep in Mind That Different Clients Will Seek Different Forms of Help from the Session

While most clients applying for help from modern SST are looking for assistance with a specific emotional or behavioural problem with which they have become stuck, this is not universally the case. Others come hoping to be listened to, have an opportunity to get matters off their chest or want to understand an issue better, among other reasons (see Dryden, 2025c). As such, the therapist needs to be prepared to offer different forms of help to different clients based on the latter's stated preferences.

While Freud did not ask any of his three single-session patients for their help preferences, he did seem to work with them in different ways. With AK, Freud focused on her symptoms, asked questions to clarify their context and offered her an explanation for her problem that she seemed to find helpful. With GM, Freud offered him a more extended opportunity to talk about his life and his rich experiences and then gave him, through interpretation, reasons for his withdrawal of libido from his wife, which GM also found useful. Finally, with ML, Freud, once alone with her, allowed her to pour out her pent-up emotional pain and then gave her specific suggestions to foster her self-development.

Keep in Mind That You Have Plenty of Time to Do the Work

Practitioners new to modern SST tend to think that there is a lot to do within the time available to them. Consequently, they tend to rush the work, and when this happens, the client tends to be left behind. In reality, if the therapist works to the client's agenda and uses time wisely to that end, then there is usually plenty of time to do the work.

The accounts available on Freud's three single sessions suggest a practitioner who takes his time. Indeed, with ML, he spends the first ten minutes in another room reading the referral letter. Additionally, with GM, the two of them take a lengthy four-hour walk through the parks and streets of Leiden, discussing Mahler's life and symptoms. The impression here is of two men taking a leisurely stroll, albeit with a specific purpose of one finding out about and helping the other.

Keep in Mind Not to Overload the Client

Another error that the therapist new to modern SST tends to make is that, given the fact that they know they may not see the client again, they want to make sure that they give the client all they can. Consequently, they overload the client both in the session and after the session when they send the client a long list of resources to consult. The result is that the client gets confused and may take little from the encounter. In modern SST, we believe that when it comes to how much to cover in a session, 'more is less' and 'less is more' and if the therapist helps the client to take away one or two points of significant learning that they can implement, then this is the hallmark of an effective single session.

There is no evidence that Freud overloaded his three single-session patients. With AL, the focus was on her symptoms and what occasioned them. With GM, they did cover a lot of ground, but had sufficient time to do so, and ML was given the opportunity to both get things off her chest and walk away with specific things to do to promote her self-development.

Keep in Mind the Importance of Negotiating an End-of-Session Goal with the Client

In modern SST, clients most often come for help with a problem they have become stuck on and for which they seek a solution (Dryden, 2025c). It is beneficial for the therapist to ask the client what they would like from the session. This is done so that if the client has unrealistic expectations for the session, these can be addressed at the outset. It is also done to provide a client-led direction for the session.

As far as I could tell, Freud did not ask any of his single-session patients what they wanted to achieve from the session. He inferred what they wanted in each case but did not ask them directly. He assumed that i) AK wanted an end to her anxiety-based symptoms; ii) GM wanted to regain his libido with his wife; and iii) ML wanted to determine the direction of her life rather than have this determined for her.

Keep in Mind the Importance of Co-creating a Therapeutic Focus and Maintaining It Once It Has Been Created

Given that the therapist in modern SST thinks that they may not see the client again (while acknowledging that they may), to increase the chances of helping the client to take away something meaningful from the session, they co-create a therapeutic focus with the client and maintain this focus throughout. The exception to this is when the client stipulates that they want to talk in an unstructured manner and for the therapist to listen to them. However, this is a rare occurrence.

There was no evidence that Freud co-created a therapeutic focus with any of his three single-session patients. However, he did engage in focused work with all of them. With AK, he concentrated throughout on her anxiety-related symptoms and helped her to understand them better. With GM, Freud was able both to learn about Mahler's life and to focus on his lack of potency with his wife, as well as on his overly restrictive behaviour towards her by preventing her from pursuing her musical interests. Remember, however, that GM and Freud had four hours together to do this. More impressively, Freud was able to allow ML to tell him about a range of situations in which she was unhappy and to focus on her desire to determine her own life. He capitalized on this desire by encouraging her to stay in the cinema when her father ordered her to leave the next time a love scene appeared on the screen.

Keep in Mind That, Unless the Client's Preference Is to the Contrary, a Single-Session Therapy Session Requires a Structure. It Has a Beginning, a Middle and an End

Following the lead of Hoyt (2025), it can be argued that a session in SST has a definite structure.

1. There is often, but not always, a pre-session phase where the client prepares themself to get the most from the session.
2. A beginning phase when the therapist and client agree to work together, co-create a focus and agree on a goal for the session.
3. A middle phase when the work of change takes place.
4. An end phase when the therapist brings the session to a suitable end and helps to restore the client's morale.
5. A post-session phase where the client reflects on what they have learned from the session, digests this learning, implements it and lets time pass before deciding whether to seek further help.

While this structure does not clearly appear in Freud's three single sessions, each one does seem to have a structure of its own.

With AK, Freud agreed to work with her, focused on her anxiety-based symptoms, made a guess that he knew the source of these symptoms, asked her many questions to clarify the thoughts and feelings related to these symptoms, listened to her elaborations and made an interpretation based on her material to help explain her symptoms – her father had sexually abused her. Freud also helped her to discover that the face she was terrified of was her father's. He was angry with her after AK informed her mother of the assaults, which led her mother to leave her father, and her father blamed AK for this. Then, the session ended.

While the structure of Freud's session with GM is less clear, we can say this. After three cancelled appointments with GM, the two finally met for a four-hour walk. During this meeting, Mahler shared details about his life and his reasons for consulting Freud. Freud then helped GM understand why he withdrew libido from his wife, and that this withdrawal, along with forcing her to abandon her musical ambitions and concentrate solely on him, had contributed to her affair with Walter Gropius. GM also discovered in the course of that discussion the factor which had prevented him from writing music of the highest rank.

Freud's session with ML had a decided structure. First, Freud removed ML's father from the session so he could talk to her alone. Second, he encouraged her to talk, and she quickly poured her heart out to him about the restrictions placed on her life by her father and grandmother after her mother died while giving birth to her. Third, when ML finally revealed her desire to watch a love scene through to its end at the cinema, something her father had hitherto prevented her from doing, Freud concentrated on this specific issue as it represented her broader wish to have greater determination over her life. He exhorted ML to remain in the cinema and defy her father the next time he wanted her to leave to avoid seeing a love scene unfold. He also made recommendations in his report to the referring doctor that she engage in activities such as skiing and dancing, which excluded him and helped her develop her independence.

Keep in Mind That a Complex Problem Can Be Addressed in SST

When therapists first encounter modern SST, they express the view that SST is not suitable for people with complex problems. This is not how those of us versed in this mode of therapy delivery view the situation. First, it depends on what the person with the complex problem wants to achieve by the end of the session. If their goal is achievable, then we will readily help them. If they want the complex problem to be solved by the end of the session, we will explain why this is unrealistic and negotiate a more doable goal with them. This often involves focusing on a specific aspect of their problem and helping them with this. The 'eating an elephant' metaphor is appropriate here. 'How do you eat an elephant? One bite at a time.' In our example, this means that a complex problem can be addressed by breaking it down into smaller, manageable steps or 'bites'. This approach makes dealing with a complex problem less intimidating for the client and more achievable over time.

Would we say that the issues that Freud's three single-session patients sought help for were simple or complex? That is a matter of opinion. I think what we can say is that, complex or straightforward, Freud helped each of his patients deal with their issues in a manageable way, and each person took away with them something meaningful and, in ML's case, life-altering.

Keep in Mind That Your Client Has Probably Attempted to Solve Their Problem Before. Look for What Has Worked, Even a Little

In modern SST, when a client seeks help with a problem, they have probably already tried to solve it before. Although none of these attempts have been wholly successful since they still have the problem, they may have done something that was somewhat helpful. If so, the therapist wants to help them identify this, build on it or incorporate it into the solution the therapist will assist them in choosing (Dryden, 2024). The SST therapist also enquires of their clients if they have solved similar problems before.

There is no evidence in Freud's work with his three single-session patients that he adopted such an approach. His stance seemed to be that he would help them find a solution going forward based on what he discovered about the problem and its relevant factors.

If Freud had adopted the practice of asking his patients about their previous attempts to solve their problem or similar problems, he would have discovered that ML had done so. She had a successful earlier experience of rebellion this time against her grandmother who was her main caregiver. In her interview with Dohler (2009), ML said:

> The other girls at school wore short dresses, while I wore a long skirt, revealing a hand-knitted, red petticoat. The other children teased me about it. So I took off my petticoat and hung it on the toilet door at school. My grandmother got it from the headmaster. After that, she never forced it on me again. That was a tremendous revolution for me, but only against my grandmother, not against my father.

If he had known about this. Freud could have used it to good effect in helping ML to defy her father.

Keep in Mind That the Client Has Strengths, Even Though They May Be Hidden from View

Another feature of modern SST is that the therapist searches for and helps the client to discover their strengths, even if these are not readily apparent. Once discovered, the therapist helps the client to draw on these strengths to address and solve their problem.

While Freud does not make a focused attempt to identify the strengths of his three single-session patients, he is aware of them. Thus, with AK. he notes, 'I am indebted to her for being so much easier to talk to than the prudish ladies in my town practice, for whom all naturalia are turpia [all natural things] are shameful' (Freud and Breuer, 2004: 135).

With GM, Ernest Jones (1955: 89) mentioned that 'Although Mahler had had no previous contact with psychoanalysis, Freud said he had never met anyone who seemed to understand it [i.e. psychoanalysis] so swiftly.' This probably encouraged Freud to be ambitious in what he covered with GM during their long walk. It may have even been a factor in why the session was so long.

With MK, Freud made no specific enquiries about her strengths. However, I believe that MK felt that Freud could see what she was capable of, and by exhorting her to defy her father, he was showing her that he thought she could do so, even if it meant keeping him in mind as she did so.

Keep in Mind That the Client Probably Has Access to a Range of Potentially Helpful External Resources

In modern SST, the therapist not only encourages the client to identify internal resources that may help them address their nominated issue, they also help the client to specific external resources that may also be helpful in this respect. These resources include other people, relevant organizations, self-help books and apps.

Obviously in Freud's day, only people known to the patient could be considered to be a helpful external resource. The only instance of this being considered by Freud is with ML, when he suggested in his report written at the end of the session that she engage in skiing and dancing, activities that would bring her into contact with people, crucial for a young woman who was very lonely.

Keep in Mind That if You Expect Change, It Often Happens

My view is that SST should only be practised by therapists who want to practise it. Sadly, this is not always the case, and particularly in agencies where SST has been introduced without the informed consent of the practitioner workforce, then this form of therapy delivery may be practised by people who think that as therapeutic change only happens over time, then very little can be achieved in a single session. Unsurprisingly, if a therapist does not expect change in SST, it tends not to occur. Whereas, if a therapist expects change to occur this has a positive effect on their behaviour with the client who benefits from this and is similarly inspired to see that change is possible and when this happens, change often occurs.

While it is difficult to say what Freud's expectations about change were in his three single sessions, my sense is that in each case he thought that he might be able to provide them with some help and as I have said earlier, in my view he did just that.

Keep in Mind to Focus First on What the Client Brings to the Table

In modern SST, the therapist generally tends to work first with constructive factors that already exist in and for the client before introducing factors that emanate from their professional knowledge and skills. The former include the client's strengths, effective problem-solving strategies that they have in their repertoire, the opposite of factors that unwittingly maintain their problem, their view of the problem and what might help address it effectively as well as others in their life who can directly support them in the change process or may inspire them as a role model. When the therapist does this, I call it working with what the client brings to the table.

There is little, if any, evidence that Freud did this in any of his single sessions discussed in this book.

Keep in Mind the Importance of Offering the Client the Opportunity to Hear What You Can Bring to the Table if What Is on the Table Is Insufficient to Effect Change

In modern SST, if what the client brings to the table is insufficient to bring about the change that they desire, then the therapist will invite them to hear the therapist's take on the problem and how the client may successfully effect change.

Freud did not invite any of his three single-session patients to bring anything to the table as discussed above. What he did was to help them based on his expert view of the nature of their problem and how it could be effectively addressed.

Keep in Mind to Check to See if Your Client Is Discussing What They Want to Discuss

In modern SST, once the therapist and client have agreed to focus on the client's nominated issue, then, as pointed out above, the therapist needs to ensure that this focus is maintained. However, sometimes it happens that the client realizes early on that they would rather focus on a different issue. Consequently, it is vital that the therapist periodically checks with the client to ensure they are still discussing what they want to discuss.

We do not know from the accounts available whether Freud made such checks with his patients. Given the fact that he generally adopted the role of expert with these patients, I would doubt whether he did this.

Keep in Mind That You Will Probably Need to Use Different Methods with Different Clients

I mentioned earlier in this chapter that clients will vary concerning the type of help that they want from a single session. Therefore, it is vital that the therapist adopt a broad helping lens rather than a narrow helping lens when practising modern SST. The same applies to the therapist's use of therapeutic methods within a particular helping mode. Thus, when helping clients who are looking to get unstuck from an emotional problem, some will benefit from cognitive methods, some from behavioural methods and yet others from imagery methods.

While Freud offered his three single-session patients different modes of help[4] – open invitations to talk with GM and ML, focused interpretative work with AK and GM and specific guidance with ML – it is difficult to judge the extent to which he used different methods within each helping mode.

Keep in Mind That It Is Important to Remain Hopeful and Trust the Client

One of the difficulties that therapists who are used to the practice of ongoing conventional therapy have when they come to practise modern SST is that they get discouraged when clients reveal the extent of their problems. In this frame of mind, they are likely to focus on what their clients can't do rather than what they can do. By contrast, therapists skilled in SST will focus on the issues their clients have come to address, even though they may reveal that they have other problems. They also trust them to be able to bring their strengths and coping abilities to their nominated issues.

I think that throughout the three sessions that Freud conducted, he remained hopeful that he would be able to help each person. Regarding the matter of trusting his patients, I find it difficult to comment. However, he did write favourably about AK's lack of prudishness in discussing her problem and about GM's ability to grasp quickly the principles of psycho-analysis. In exhorting ML to defy her father in the cinema, I believe he was saying to her implicitly that she could do this even if she needed the additional help of keeping his image in mind when doing so.

Keep in Mind That if Your Client Is Seeking Help for a Problem, You Will Probably Both Need to Be Solution-Focused

While clients may seek modern SST for several reasons, they often come because they feel stuck with a problem, and when this is the case, they are looking for a solution to help them get unstuck and move forward. This involves them both adopting a solution-focused approach to the session. A solution is something the client does to render the problem a non-problem, and as such, it is helpful if the client can see what their life would be like if they did not have the problem, so that they have something to aim for.

Freud's single sessions were characterized by his taking the lead in finding a solution to his patients' problems. With AK and GM, this involved Freud offering them an understanding of their symptoms, which made sense to them. Whether these explanations were true was less important than the fact that the patients could emotionally resonate with them.

With ML, Freud's proposed solution was different. According to Roos (2016: 297):

> He [Freud] told her that she was now 18 years old and thus an adult. And furthermore – this was less a prescription than an appeal – 'Being an adult means overcoming complaints and asserting what it means to be a person. Having desires. Contemplating dissent. Asking why things are as they are and not simply accepting

everything in silence. Asserting with determination, firmness, and calm what one considers truly important.' And, he prescribed in no uncertain terms, 'the next time there's a kissing scene in a movie, you stay seated!' I am telling you, 'You stay seated!' Pause. Deep eyes. Finally, 'Have me in mind!'

Keep in Mind the Value of Rehearsing a Solution

If you wanted to buy a new car, you would probably take it out for a test drive before committing yourself to making a purchase. Similarly, in modern SST once a client has chosen a solution, it is helpful for the therapist to encourage them to rehearse it to see what it feels like and if they can imagine implementing it.

Freud did not do this in any of his sessions.

Keep in Mind the Value of Action Planning

In modern SST, once the client has selected a solution, it is helpful for the therapist to encourage them to develop an action plan for its implementation. This involves the client specifying:

- *Why* they are going to implement the solution.
- *When* they are going to implement it.
- *Where* they are going to implement it.
- *What* do they need to face when they implement it.
- *Who* needs to be present when they implement it.
- *How often* they are going to implement it.

The only time Freud did anything that resembled action planning was when he said to ML with respect to her wish to see a love scene through to its end in the cinema, ' "[T]he next time there's a kissing scene in a movie, you stay seated!" I am telling you, "You stay seated!" "Have me in mind!" ' (Roos, 2016: 297).

Keep in Mind That All You May Need to Do Is to Get the Client Moving, and That Small May Be Beautiful

'A journey of a thousand miles begins with a single step' is a proverb from Lao Tzu's Tao Te Ching that illustrates the aim of modern SST. This suggests that the therapist's primary role in the session is to assist the client in beginning the process of change by taking a small step forward.

I think Freud demonstrated this point with ML when he exhorted her to defy her father in the cinema when he ordered her to leave with him when a love scene came on to the screen.

Keep in Mind That Change Occurs in Different Forms

Psychological change may happen for a variety of reasons. Thus, a person may solve their problem, for example, because:

1. They have changed their attitude toward an adversity (attitude change).
2. They have made a more constructive inference of the adversity (inference change).
3. They have made a behaviour change in the face of the adversity (behaviour change).
4. They have changed their relationship with the way they have responded to the adversity (response relationship change).
5. They have put the adversity and their response to it in a completely different frame (frame change).
6. They have changed their environment for the better, so they no longer face the adversity (environmental change).
7. A combination of the above.

While the modern SST therapist may have their own view about which form of change will benefit the client the most, the client is deemed to be the best judge of what is best for them.

In my view, Freud was not overly concerned about the form of change experienced by his single-session patients, only that such change occurred. He did not know, and neither do we, *how* AK or GM changed as a result of their meeting with him. Indeed, we have only sketchy reports that they found the session helpful.

With ML, the situation is different as we have her own report of the session and its aftermath. She claimed to have changed profoundly after meeting with Freud. Specifically and directly following her session, ML changed her behaviour (e.g., by resisting her father's attempts to remove her from the cinema when a love scene came on screen and by going skiing and dancing, activities that did not involve her father). More generally, by her own account, she became more independent and self-determining as a person. In my view, this points to both attitude and behavioural change.

Keep in Mind the Usefulness of Asking Your Client to Summarize the Session as You Reach the End of the Session

In modern SST, helping a client to develop an action plan signals that the end of the session is approaching. When this happens, the therapist keeps in mind that it is vital to ask the client to summarize their work together. The client should summarize the work rather than the therapist, because this shows what the client has found helpful about the session and helps frame what they are going to take away from it.

As far as we know, Freud did not ask his single-session patients to summarize what they covered in the session.

Keep in Mind the Helpfulness of Encouraging Your Client to Specify Their Takeaway(s) from the Session

If the therapist and client have collaborated on finding a solution to the client's nominated problem, this solution should be part of what the client takes away from the session. However, the client may also take away other learning points. Therefore, the modern SST therapist explicitly asks the client for their personal key takeaways from the session. The therapist is aware that the more the client tries to take away, the less they may actually retain. Consequently, if the client lists multiple takeaways, the therapist encourages them to prioritize these, so they can later focus on no more than three key points.

Again, as far as we know, Freud did not ask his single-session patients to specify their key takeaways from the session.

Keep in Mind the Value of Encouraging Your Client to Generalize Their Learning, if Possible

In modern SST, we not only want the client to leave with a specific plan to address their nominated problem, if that has been the focus of the work, but also to be able to generalize their learning to other areas of their life whenever possible. Therefore, if feasible and if it does not detract from the work done in the session, the therapist will encourage the client to consider how they might generalize their insights to maximize the benefits of the session.

Yet again, as far as we know, Freud did not ask his single-session patients to specify how they would generalize what they learned from the session to other areas of their lives.

Keep in Mind That the Benefits That Your Client Derives from the Session Will Be Mainly Achieved Outside the Session

Very occasionally in modern SST, the client experiences maximum benefit from the session. Their problem has been solved. When this occurs, and it is not common, it is because the therapist has helped the client to make a frame change (see above), and such a change does not need to be practised after the session. However, most of the benefit that the client gains from the session is realized after it has finished. This is why, for example, the therapist helps the client to develop an action plan to implement their chosen solution.

It is clear that Freud was focused on helping his single-session patients in the time he had with them, and there is little indication that, with AK and GM, he thought about what they could do after the session to achieve the session's maximum benefits. With ML, Freud was thinking about what she could do after the session. This is shown in his exhortation for her to defy her father in the cinema and in his recommendation that she should take up skiing and dancing. Freud knew that in ML's case, the session he had with her was the prelude to change. He did not think it was sufficient to effect change. It is not clear that Freud made such a distinction in his work with AK and GM.

Keep in Mind That the Best Time for Your Client to Judge if They Need More Help Is When They Have Had an Opportunity to Reflect on What They Learned from the Session, to Digest This Learning, to Implement What They Learned and to Let Time Pass a Little

As we have seen in modern SST, the therapist collaborates with the client to help take away their stated wants from the session, with the understanding that they can request additional support later if necessary. This generally means that the therapist does not offer the client another appointment at the end of the session they have just completed. The client should gain the maximum benefit from the session by reflecting on what they've learned, processing this knowledge, applying it, and observing the outcomes. After a suitable period, as determined by the client themself, they will recognize whether the session has met their needs or if further assistance is required.

As already discussed, there is no evidence that Freud believed he would consult with any of his three single-session patients again. If he had, my best guess is that he would have scheduled an appointment to see them at the end of their session, as would have been the custom.

Keep in Mind the Importance of Ending the Session Well so That the Client Leaves the Session with Their Morale Restored

Jerome Frank (1961) argued that while clients seek therapy for various reasons, most of them arrive in a state of demoralization. One of the aims of modern SST is to help clients leave the session with their morale restored, at least in part, hopeful that things can change for them after the session. This means that it is important for the therapist to conclude the session effectively, ensuring that the client has expressed everything they wanted to say and asked everything they wanted to ask.

Did Freud end his single sessions well? We do not know the answer in the cases of AK and GM. In the case of ML, as reported by Roos (2016) in his interview with the patient, the end came when Freud looked deeply into her eyes and exhorted her to defy her father while keeping him in mind. If this was, in fact, the way Freud's session with ML ended, then it was very dramatic and would have likely had a lasting impact, which we know that it did.

Keep in Mind the Value of Taking Nothing for Granted in SST

In modern SST, it is sometimes remarked that it is difficult to predict what a client has taken away from the session. Sometimes the therapist has been happy with a session only to learn that the client did not find it helpful, and at other times the therapist has despaired about a session only to learn how useful the client found it. Consequently, SST therapists do the best they can and take nothing for granted.

Freud hoped AK would derive some benefit from their conversation. He had had reports that he had achieved much with GM. But I don't think Freud, in his wildest dreams, would have thought that his 45-minute session with ML would have had the lasting impact on her and her life that it did.

Keep in Mind That It Is OK if the Client Chooses to Seek Further Help, and It Is OK if They Don't

As already mentioned, in modern SST, the client is put centre stage. They lead the process and make the key decisions, such as whether to seek further help later. In conventional therapy, the therapist may doubt themself if the client chooses not to return after their first session. Ideally, the SST therapist does not have the same doubts. They are comfortable if the client seeks further help and comfortable if they don't. This does not mean that they can rest on their laurels. A good SST therapist seeks to improve their practice and seeks supervision to that end. However, it does mean that they acknowledge that whatever the client chooses to do regarding further help-seeking is acceptable.

As we have observed, Freud likely regarded these three single sessions as 'one-off' sessions where he would not see the person again. However, if ML had asked for more assistance and her father had supported her in this, Freud probably would have provided it, given that the original meeting took place in his consulting room. In the cases of AK and GM, where sessions took place outside his consulting room while he was on holiday, he would likely have arranged for them to receive further help in their location if they had requested it.

In this chapter, I have discussed the elements of the SST mindset and assessed how Freud fared on each element. In the concluding chapter, I will make some final reflections on Freud's single-session work and its role in the development of what I have called here modern SST.

Notes

1 Recall that Freud's session with AK took place in 1893, his session with GM took place in 1910, and his session with ML took place in 1936.
2 See note 4 at the end of Chapter 4.
3 See note 3 at the end of Chapter 3.
4 The suitability of these helping modes was determined by Freud and not his patients.

6 Final Reflections

In his seminal book on SST, Talmon (1990: 3) says the following: 'To the best of my knowledge, the "founder" of SST was none other than Sigmund Freud, better known as the founder of the longest form of therapy, psychoanalysis.' Talmon knew about Freud's session with AK and GM, but the interview with ML, which was the third of Freud's single sessions, came out in 2006, 16 years after the publication of Talmon's book. If we take the three sessions together, I would put it a little differently than Talmon. I would say that these three sessions constitute the origins of SST. The term 'founder' seems to describe a person who intentionally establishes a particular approach to something. By this definition, Freud is not the founder of SST since it seems clear to me that he was not intentionally trying to establish SST as a mode of therapy delivery. Rather, he responded to the situations presented to him.

In the previous chapter, I briefly discussed 47 elements of the single-session mindset and put forward my views about how Freud fared on each element. Let me pull out some strands from this discussion and from the description and analysis of the three single sessions (as presented in Chapters 2, 3 and 4) to provide some reflections on Freud's work in the area.

Flexible Freud

In my view, the three single sessions that Freud conducted that I discussed in this book showed Freud's flexibility. First, he was prepared to interrupt his holiday to discuss with a young, sullen-looking woman (AK) her anxiety-based symptoms in a mountain

DOI: 10.4324/9781003639633-6

range there and then. I wonder how many therapists would have done so today. Second, he was again prepared to interrupt his holiday to talk to a famous composer and conductor (GM) who had made and cancelled three appointments before finally consulting Freud. On the fourth attempt, the two men spoke for four hours while walking through the parks and streets of Leiden in the Netherlands. Finally, in his consulting room, Freud departed from his usual longer-term psychoanalytic work to give another young woman (MK) an opportunity to tell him about her very lonely and restricted life, and he ends the session by encouraging her to defy her father and watch a love scene in the cinema from beginning to end.

Many modern psychoanalytic therapists would regard such practices almost as acts of heresy, but Freud knew what each of his patients needed and was confident enough in his own therapeutic skin to offer them each personalized care, even if this meant departing from standard practice.

Freud's Working Alliance with His Patients

In Chapter 1, I mentioned that the working alliance between the therapist and client four constituents: bonds, views, goals and tasks. I said there:

> a good working alliance occurs when the therapist and client have a good enough collaborative bond, share views on matters related to the client's problems and their remediation, agree on the goals of therapy, and agree on the tasks needed to help the client achieve their goals. Such agreements can be either explicit or implicit.

What was the working alliance like between Freud and his single-session patients?[1]

Bonds

In my view, Freud established a strong working alliance with all three single-session patients. While each relationship was different, Freud employed his role as an expert to facilitate the therapy process in each case. Thus, AK was impressed that he was a doctor, and GM was impressed by his reputation and the insights he offered. With ML,

Freud showed that he was someone worth listening to after dismissing her father, allowing him to speak to her alone.

However, other elements of the therapeutic bond could be discerned in Freud's single-session work. Thus, he listened well to all three patients – a fact emphasized in Roos's (2006, 2016) translated title of his interview with ML, 'The Good Listener' – and encouraged them to talk in focused (i.e., with AK) and more open ways (with GM and ML).

I think all three patients felt that Freud was keen to help them and understood them. ML stressed the latter feature in her interviews about her session with Freud, 70 years after it took place (Roos, 2006, 2016; Dohler, 2009).

In conclusion, my view is that Freud intuitively knew the type of therapeutic bond to form with each of his patients and was successful in doing so in all three cases.

Views

Freud was confident that he knew what ailed each of his patients and how to help them, and his patients generally went along with his approach in each case. So, it is possible to argue that Freud and his patients shared views on matters related to the patients' problems and their remediation. However, in each case, his patient deferred to his expertise. He never explicitly asked them for their views on these matters.

Goals

Freud never explicitly asked his patients what they wanted to achieve from their single meeting. He assumed that each had a problem for which they wanted help and proceeded on that basis. However, we can say the following about each patient's implicit goals.

1. AK's goal seemed to be not having her distressing anxiety-related symptoms.
2. GM wanted to regain potency with his wife.
3. ML did not seek help from Freud. She was taken to see him and did not know, at the outset, what kind of doctor he was. However, as she revealed in the session. ML wanted to determine her own life and be understood by someone.

Again, I would argue that Freud shared these goals and that he and each of his patients were working toward a common end.

Tasks

Freud's therapeutic tasks were somewhat different for each patient, and once again, each seemed happy to go along with him and respond to his way of working. With AK, Freud was very focused on her symptoms, quickly determined that her anxiety was hysterical in nature, developed a hypothesis based on his then-current view of the causes of hysteria, found evidence to support this and put this to AK, who seemed to accept it.

While Freud's tasks with AK were focused, his work with GM and ML were both broad and focused at different times, and both seemed to work well with these shifts. GM was able to recount his life story and focus on his loss of libido for his wife. ML was able to respond to Freud's general invitation to talk, during which she expressed her pent-up feelings of loneliness and of living a highly restricted life. She was then able to work with Freud in a more focused way, when he encouraged her to be an adult and defy her father in the cinema as previously discussed.

In conclusion, it is my view that Freud developed and maintained a good enough working alliance with each of his single-session patients and that this contributed to any benefits that they derived from their single consultation with Freud.

An Unhurried Freud Does Not Overload His Patients

Two common errors committed by those new to SST are rushing and overloading the client. In this respect, the therapist who is new to SST is a bit like a rabbit caught in the headlights. They know that they may have only one chance to help someone and only a very limited time to do so, and respond poorly to this. Thus, they may rush through the session, often leaving their client behind and confused. In doing so, they underestimate just how long 50 minutes can be.[2] They also respond by cramming too much into the session, and afterwards, they may email the client with additional 'helpful' links to further resources. Here, the client is often overwhelmed by so much material that they again end up confused. By contrast, a skilled SST therapist works at a steady pace with each client, focusing on one or two key points, so that the client leaves the session with a clear sense of a path forward that they are confident they can take.

Reading the different accounts of Freud's single-session work, I get the impression that Freud worked in an unhurried way with each of his patients. Although he covered a lot of ground with each person, none of them seemed overwhelmed, and each seemed to take away something useful to them, and in ML's case, that something was life-changing.

Different Strokes for Different Folks

One of the key features of modern SST is that it is client-centred. Although there are specific approaches to SST, most SST therapists prefer to customize their work to suit the unique goals and situations of their clients, drawing on insights from various therapeutic methods as needed. Therefore, single-session therapists tend to bring a 'different strokes for different folks' perspective to this mode of therapy delivery. This perspective is also evident in Freud's work on SST. As discussed, he tailored his approach for each single-session patient.

For AK, his focus was on her anxiety symptoms, using precise questioning influenced by his theory that, in girls, such anxiety results from the overwhelming horror experienced when a virginal mind confronts sexuality for the first time.

For GM, he had both a broad and a narrow focus, learning about GM's life when adopting a broad focus and helping him to understand better his loss of libido with his wife when adopting a narrow focus.

With ML, his approach was different again, first allowing her to get her pent-up feelings of loneliness and frustration off her chest before encouraging her to determine her own life as an adult by defying her father and taking up activities which did not involve him, where she could meet and interact with people of her own age.

A Single Therapeutic Encounter Can Be Profoundly Transformative

While modern SST therapists tend to be rather conservative in what they consider their clients can achieve from a single session, the case of ML reminds us that sometimes a single encounter can have transformative effects that are remembered many years later.

Conclusion

Freud's three single sessions, as discussed in this book, spanned a period of 43 years (from 1893 to 1936). Given this timeframe, it would be unusual to expect Freud to think of adopting a single-session approach to therapy, and for this reason, I don't think that Freud can be properly thought of as the 'founder' of SST as suggested by Talmon (1990). While it would be useful to speculate on the development of psychotherapy if Freud had applied SST more systematically to his work, this is beyond my brief.

Instead, I think what we can say is that the origins of SST can be seen in the three single sessions discussed in this book. We can also say that these sessions reveal Freud to be flexible enough to work in unusual settings, at unusual times, and to have confidence in himself as a therapist, as well as the skills to engage quickly with different clients who have varying needs.

I end on a personal note. When I began planning this book, I was concerned that I would not have much to say about Freud's work in this area. Having finished the book, not only have I found much to say, but much to admire as well.

Notes

1 I discussed this issue regarding each of Freud's patients in Chapters 2, 3 and 4. In this chapter, I will make some overall reflections.

2 For the sake of argument, I assume here that a single session lasts for 50 minutes. In reality, it is often shorter, and sometimes longer.

References

Appignanesi, L. and Forrester, J. (2005). *Freud's Women*. Weidenfeld & Nicholson.

Bobele, M. and Slive, A. (eds) (2025). *Implementing Single-Session Psychotherapy: When No Appointment Is Necessary*. Routledge.

Bordin, E.S. (1979). The generalizability of the psychoanalytic concept of the working alliance. *Psychotherapy: Theory, Research and Practice*, 16(3), 252–60.

Brown, G.S. and Jones, E.R. (2005). Implementing a feedback system in a managed care environment: What are patients teaching us? *Journal of Clinical Psychology*, 61, 187–98.

Cohen, Y. (2016). The enveloping gaze. *Psychoanalytic Perspectives*, 13, 36–330.

Dohler, C. (2009, 27 March). Wir haben uns immerzu in die augen geshaut und er hat sehr viel gelächelt [We looked into each other's eyes the whole time and he smiled a lot] (Interview with Margarerthe Lutz). *Süddeutsche Zeitung Magazin*, 13. http://sz-magazin.sueddeutsche.de/texte/anzeigen/28738/Er-hat-sehr-viel-gelaechelt

Dryden, W. (2006). *Counselling in a Nutshell*. Sage.

Dryden, W. (2011). *Counselling in a Nutshell*. 2nd edition. Sage.

Dryden, W. (2020). *Single-Session Coaching and One-at-a-Time Coaching: Distinctive Features*. Routledge.

Dryden, W. (2022). *Single-Session Therapy: Responses to Frequently Asked Questions*. Routledge.

Dryden, W. (2024). *Single-Session Therapy: 100 Key Points and Techniques*. 2nd edition. Routledge.

Dryden, W. (2025a). *A Critique of Irvin D. Yalom's Single-Session Consultations: It Is the Relationship That Heals*. Routledge.

Dryden, W. (2025b). *50 Not Out! A Half Century of Working in the Field of Counselling and Psychotherapy*. Onlinevents Publications.

Dryden, W. (2025c). Bringing a single-session mindset to counselling in an online health service in the UK. In F. Cannistrà and M.F. Hoyt (eds), *Single Session Therapies: Why and How One-at-a-Time Mindsets Are Effective* (pp. 124–36). Routledge.

Frank, J. (1961). *Persuasion and Healing: A Comparative Study of Psychotherapy*. Johns Hopkins University Press.

Freud, S. and Breuer, J. (1895). *Studien Über Hysterie*. Deuticke.

Freud, S. and Breuer, J. (2004). *Studies in Hysteria*. Penguin.

Hoyt, M.F. (2025). *Single Session Therapy: A Clinical Introduction to Principles and Practices*. Routledge.

Hoyt, M.F. and Talmon, M.F. (2014). What the literature says: An annotated bibliography. In M.F. Hoyt and M. Talmon (eds), *Capturing the Moment: Single Session Therapy and Walk-In Services* (pp. 487–516). Crown House Publishing.

Jones, E. (1955). *The Life and Work of Sigmund Freud, Volume 2: Years of Maturity. 1909–1919*. Basic Books.

Kuehn, J.L. (1965). Encounter at Leyden: Gustav Mahler consults Sigmund Freud. *Psychoanalytic Review*, 52, 345–65.

Mahler, A.M. (1946). *Gustav Mahler: Memories and Letters*. Viking Press.

Mahrer, A.R. (ed.) (1967). *The Goals of Psychotherapy*. Appleton-Century.

Porter, S., Pitt, T., Eubank, M., Butt, J. and Thomas, O. (2024). An expert understanding of the single-session mindset. *Journal of Systemic Therapies*, 43(3).

Rogers, C.R. (1957). The necessary and sufficient conditions of therapeutic personality change. *Journal of Consulting Psychology*, 21, 95–103.

Roos, P. (2006, 27 April). Der große zuhörer. *Die Zeit*, 18. Zeitverlag Gerd Bucerius. https://www.zeit.de/2006/18/Freuds_Patientin

Roos, P. (2016). The great listener. *Psychoanalytic Perspectives*, 13, 294–9.

Sabbiadini, A. (1992). 'The truth is, sir, my nerves are bad': Reflections on Freud's case of Katharina. *British Journal of Psychotherapy*, 9(2), 157–68.

Simon, G.E., Imel, Z.E., Ludman, E.J. and Steinfeld, B.J. (2012). Is dropout after a first psychotherapy visit always a bad outcome? *Psychiatric Services*, 63(7), 705–7.

Slavin, J.H. (2016). 'I never felt I should think about Freud': From authority to liberation in psychoanalytic work. *Psychoanalytic Perspectives*, 13, 321–5.

Slavin, J.H. and Rahmani, M. (2016). Those 45 minutes changed my life: The meeting of Sigmund Freud and Margarethe Lutz. *Psychoanalytic Perspectives*, 13, 291–3.

Strong, S.R. and Claiborn, C.D. (1982). *Change through Interaction*. Wiley.

Swales, P.J. (1988). Freud, Katharina and the first 'wild analysis'. In P.E. Stepansky (ed.), *Freud Appraisals and Reappraisals: Contributions to Freud Studies*, Volume 3. Analytic Press.

Talmon, M. (1990). *Single-Session Therapy: Maximising the Effect of the First (and Often Only) Therapeutic Encounter*. Jossey-Bass.

van Amorongen, M. (1992). *Mahler's Mater Dolorosa*. Arbeiderspers.

Yalom, I.D. and Yalom, B (2024). *Hour of the Heart: Connecting in the Here and Now*. Piatkus.

Young, J. (2018). SST: The misunderstood gift that keeps on giving. In M.F. Hoyt, M. Bobele, A. Slive, J. Young and M. Talmon (eds), *Single-Session Therapy by Walk-In or Appointment: Administrative, Clinical, and Supervisory Aspects of One-at-a-Time Services* (pp. 40–58). Routledge.

Index

Note: End of chapter notes are denoted by a letter 'n' between the page and note number.

For Product Safety Concerns and Information please contact our EU representative GPSR@taylorandfrancis.com Taylor & Francis Verlag GmbH, Kaufingerstraße 24, 80331 München, Germany